PHILADELPHIA THEATERS
A Pictorial Architectural History

IRVIN R. GLAZER

A Joint Publication of
THE ATHENAEUM OF PHILADELPHIA
and
DOVER PUBLICATIONS, INC.
NEW YORK

To my children
Judy and Mollie
with affection

Copyright

Copyright © 1994 by The Athenaeum of Philadelphia.
All rights reserved under Pan American and International Copyright
Conventions.

Published in Canada by General Publishing Company, Ltd., 30
Lesmill Road, Don Mills, Toronto, Ontario.
Published in the United Kingdom by Constable and Company, Ltd.,
3 The Lanchesters, 162–164 Fulham Palace Road, London W6 9ER.

Bibliographical Note

Philadelphia Theaters: A Pictorial Architectural History is a new work,
first published jointly by The Athenaeum of Philadelphia and Dover
Publications, Inc., New York, in 1994.

Book design by Carol Belanger Grafton

Library of Congress Cataloging-in-Publication Data

Glazer, Irvin R., 1922–
    Philadelphia theaters : a pictorial architectural history / Irvin R.
Glazer.
        p.   cm.
    Published in conjunction with an exhibition held at the Athenaeum
of Philadelphia, Sept. 26, 1994–Feb. 3, 1995, including its Irvin R.
Glazer collection.
    ISBN 0-486-27833-6
    1. Theater architecture—Pennsylvania—Philadelphia—Exhibi-
tions. 2. Architecture, Modern—20th century—Pennsylvania—Phila-
delphia—Exhibitions. 3. Theaters—Decoration—Pennsylvania—
Philadelphia—Exhibitions. 4. Glazer, Irvin R., 1922-   —Art
collections—Exhibitions. 5. Art—Private collections—Pennsylvania—
Philadelphia—Exhibitions. 6. Art—Pennsylvania—Philadelphia—
Exhibitions. 7. Athenaeum of Philadelphia—Exhibitions. 8. Phila-
delphia (Pennsylvania)—Buildings, structures, etc.—Exhibitions. I.
Athenaeum of Philadelphia. II. Title.
NA6830.G578 1994
725′.822′097481107474811—dc20   94-27456
                                                                    CIP

Manufactured in the United States of America
Dover Publications, Inc., 31 East 2nd Street, Mineola, N.Y. 11501

Contents

Preface

THE publication of this book is coordinated with the opening of an exhibition entitled "Behind the Marquee: Philadelphia Theatre Buildings, 1900–1932" at The Athenaeum of Philadelphia (September 26, 1994, through February 3, 1995). The purpose of both the exhibition and book is to call attention to the rich visual resources available at The Athenaeum for the study of theater architecture and decoration, particularly in Philadelphia during the first decades of the twentieth century.

In his foreword, Bruce Laverty, Gladys Brooks Curator of Architecture at The Athenaeum of Philadelphia, discusses how the theater-architecture collection relates to the overall collecting emphasis of the institution. For those readers who are as yet unfamiliar with The Athenaeum, I should say that it is a member-supported library and historic-site museum with research collections founded in 1814 to collect materials "connected with the history and antiquities of America, and the useful arts, and generally to disseminate useful knowledge." The collections are housed in a handsomely restored and expanded National Historic Landmark building located near Independence Hall.

The research library is freely open to serious investigators, and it annually attracts thousands of readers: graduate students and senior scholars, architects, interior designers, museum curators and private owners of historic buildings. While not publicly funded, The Athenaeum provides a rich resource for readers on architecture and interior-design history who are able to arrange a visit to Philadelphia.

I particularly want to thank Irvin R. Glazer and Henry J. Magaziner, who gave many of the photographs and drawings reproduced here, and Frank C. P. McGlinn for his wise counsel. Most of the credit for successfully attending to the thousand tasks involved in organizing the exhibition and this book goes to Bruce Laverty and his associate Rebecca J. Mayne. Thanks also goes to Dena Dannenberg for volunteering countless hours in the processing of the Glazer Collection. Finally, we are grateful to John Grafton and the staff of Dover Publications, who supported the project from the beginning.

ROGER W. MOSS
Executive Director

Theater Materials at The Athenaeum of Philadelphia

FOR many years, The Athenaeum has actively collected, conserved and made available to the public original materials documenting the architectural history of Philadelphia and the mid-Atlantic region. The foremost component of the research collections are the approximately 120,000 architectural drawings (1795–1980) that represent the work of more than 500 American architects. With a supporting reference library of more than 50,000 volumes, 25,000 photographs and several million manuscripts, The Athenaeum is a major resource for preservationists, students of building history and architects.

It was with considerable pleasure, therefore, that The Athenaeum received the Irvin R. Glazer Theater Collection, highlights of which are shown throughout the pages that follow. The collection represents a lifetime of collecting and research by the donor. Included in the 70 cubic feet of material are original photographs, dedication programs, playbills, news clippings and correspondence relating to nearly 1,000 theater buildings. Although the bulk of the collection documents Philadelphia theaters, there is extensive information on dozens of New York theaters as well as playhouses and motion-picture houses throughout the world. One component that makes the Glazer Collection particularly rich is the hundreds of studio photographs from the prolific architectural firm of William H. Hoffman and Paul J. Henon, Jr., who designed 32 theater buildings in Philadelphia, including their masterpiece, the Mastbaum (1929). The Glazer Collection is also supported by the photo and inventory files of the Stanley-Warner Company, the leading motion-picture distributor in Philadelphia during the first half of the twentieth century.

Mr. Glazer's gift also included 2,000 slides—many taken by himself—documenting both interiors and exteriors of past and present theaters, and a library of theater-building history. Long after the era of the great motion-picture palaces has passed from living memory, the Glazer Collection at The Athenaeum will provide a priceless resource to students of theater history and architecture. Unless otherwise noted, all images in this book are from that collection.

The Glazer Collection joins The Athenaeum's already substantial holdings documenting Philadelphia's architectural theater heritage. One of the earliest Athenaeum architectural drawings for a theater building in Philadelphia is John Skirving's design for the interior of the Musical Fund Hall (c. 1843). The Athenaeum also preserves two sets of 1854 competition drawings for the Academy of Music, one by Edwin Forrest Durang and the other by John Notman. Under a long-term loan agreement, the Historical Society of Pennsylvania has placed at The Athenaeum two additional sets of drawings for the Academy: Stephen D. Button's unsuccessful competition entry, as well as the winning Napoleon LeBrun and Gustav Runge drawings.

———

Several early-twentieth-century theaters are also documented in the archives of the Ballinger Company and of Hodgens & Hill, architects. The Athenaeum maintains a set of stunning Art Moderne designs from 1932 by Voorhees, Gmelin & Walker for a proposed, but unexecuted, Concert Hall for the Philadelphia Orchestra at Logan Circle.

———

Apart from the Glazer gift, the largest cache of original theater materials at The Athenaeum is the Magaziner Collection; it contains more than 500 original architectural drawings documenting eighteen motion-picture theaters that Louis Magaziner (1878–1956) and his partners designed between 1911 and 1950, including the Uptown, Ogontz, Arcadia and Midway. The Magaziner Collection is one of the most complete at The Athenaeum, including working drawings, fully rendered presentation drawings, photographs, specifications, building agreements and correspondence.

———

The Glazer Collection and the other collections mentioned here are available for research. Appointments may be made by writing to the Curator of Architecture, Athenaeum of Philadelphia, 219 South Sixth Street, Philadelphia, PA 19106.

BRUCE LAVERTY
Gladys Brooks Curator of Architecture

A Brief History of Philadelphia Theater Buildings to 1900

THE main body of this book provides a photographic record of the great Philadelphia theater palaces of the twentieth century. It is the aim of this introduction to provide a historical context for that material by reviewing the development of Philadelphia theaters from their earliest period until the end of the nineteenth century.

The Colonial City

In all things intellectual and artistic—including the theater and theater buildings—Philadelphia was the premier city of the English colonies in the New World. Philadelphia's preeminence as a theatrical center lasted until 1830, after which New York City became the entertainment capital (although Philadelphia continued as an important theater town). In a hostile atmosphere wherein government, press and clergy degraded the players and even forbade the existence of theaters, most thespians eventually emigrated to New York, leaving Philadelphia to establish itself as the leading tryout town for major shows as well as an important residential center.

As Philadelphia grew from a haven for religious exiles into a thriving city, the Quaker ideal of simplicity was continually at odds with the theater trades. Early laws sought to prohibit any public assembly that might undermine the moral order. Eventually the increasing non-Quaker presence overcame this opposition, but the transition was gradual.

Philadelphia's earliest theatrical venues were situated outside the city limits to avoid the fines and imprisonment mandated by the Quaker civil authorities. The best location was across the city's southern boundary, South Street. Despite constant opposition, attempts to establish theaters within Philadelphia proper resumed after each prohibitive law was passed. The efforts of early theater organizers were not without public support: three times between 1700 and 1718, laws prohibiting theatrical events were repealed by popular mandate.

In 1723, responding to complaints that a theatrical company was performing on a stage outside the city limits, Mayor James Logan asserted that "the sober people" wished him to repress these activities. In 1724, the *American Weekly Mercury* reported an acrobatic show presented at the New Booth Theatre in Society Hill, the first recorded local-area theater. Featured was a young girl who "danced and capered upon a straight rope." The only clue the account gives to the theatrical setting is a price list for seats on the stage and in the pit and gallery.

The curtain finally rose before a dramatic stage within the city's borders in 1749, when William Plumstead transformed his large warehouse, a lofty glazed-brick building on Water Street between Pine and Lombard, into a makeshift theater. Plumstead's venture met with strong religious opposition, forcing the suspension of productions in February 1750. Nevertheless, Plumstead, a Quaker turned Anglican, became mayor that same year, and in 1754 reopened his theater, newly equipped with a stage, pit, gallery and boxes.

On June 25, 1759, the first Philadelphia-area theater specifically constructed as such opened just outside the city limits, at the southwest corner of South and Hancock Streets. Named the Theatre on Society Hill, the modest frame structure was, like earlier playhouses, a subject of controversy: the *Philadelphia Chronicle*, between June and December of 1759, published a long series of letters decrying the "blasphemous spectacles, wanton amours, profane jests and impure passions" offered. The Society Hill lasted only one season; it is recorded that over the proscenium arch was printed the motto *Totus mundus agit histrionem* (The whole world acts a part).

The first successful theater building in the English colonies, the Southwark, opened on November 12, 1766, on the south side of South Street, west of Fourth. The American Company, headed by theater manager and amateur architect David Douglass, operated the theater. Growing public acceptance of the stage at this time is indicated by the appearance of theater program ads for the Southwark in the *Pennsylvania Gazette* and the *Pennsylvania Chronicle*.

The completed theater measured 95 by 55 feet. The foundation and first-floor exterior were of rough cast brick; the second floor was of wood-frame construction, painted bright red, with a steep sloped roof straddled by a cupola in the center. The three windows at the second level were rectangular, but they were painted to give a

The Southwark Theatre, South Street west of Fourth Street, was the first permanent theater building in the English colonies. Construction was supervised by actor David Douglass, and the Southwark opened in 1766. It ceased operations in 1817. It stood on the south side of the street, just outside the colonial city's limits, thereby avoiding Philadelphia's anti-theater laws.

Palladian effect via an artificial arch. Colonial playgoers had to trudge through the mud of South Street to enter through one of the two flush entrance doors. The roof leaked and winter customers brought their own small foot stoves. The stage was lighted by exposed oil lamps. Sightlines from the boxes were blocked by large wooden pillars supporting the upper tier and roof. The front benches in the gallery were the best seats in the theater.

During the British Army's occupation of Philadelphia in 1777–1778 the theater building was used as a hospital, and after the Revolution the Southwark continued to be used for legitimate theater productions until 1817 (although in 1787 it was renamed "The Opera House"—an appellation that was given to hundreds of halls across the country in an attempt to avoid the socially unacceptable connotations of the term "theater"). During the Federal period the stage box on the east side was equipped with cushioned seats and red draperies, decorated with the coat of arms of the United States and reserved for President Washington, a frequent attendee. The theater's director, Thomas Wignell, would await Washington's arrival at the door of the box in full dress and white wig, carrying two silver candlesticks, and would ceremoniously conduct him to his seat.

The Federal City

In 1789, the Pennsylvania legislature repealed the last law prohibiting theater performances, prompting the erection of the first Chestnut Street Theatre. Construction, from designs modeled after a theater in Bath, England, commenced in 1791 and was completed in 1793. The yellow-fever epidemic, however, prevented the opening of the theater until February 17, 1794.

The Chestnut was the most lavish theater in the United States, and its location at Sixth and Chestnut Streets was prestigious, being located diagonally across Chestnut Street from the United States Capitol. Early prints show a handsome facade with a steeply inclined wood awning, enclosed on both sides and extending to iron supports mid-sidewalk. The area beneath was open

only to the street side. An 1805 alteration by architect Benjamin Henry Latrobe (1764–1820) removed the awning and added ten Corinthian columns at the building line, which were flanked in turn by two projecting 15-foot wings, creating an open court in front of the original building. The facade was further ornamented by figures of Comedy and Tragedy carved by sculptor William Rush. Some marble was used, but the predominant building material was red brick.

Flickering candlelight from numerous chandeliers reflected against three horseshoe galleries and a parquet of 13 rows that together accommodated an audience of 1,165. The parquet originally consisted of long curved benches without back supports. The stage was 36 feet wide and 71 feet deep. The Chestnut and New York's Park Theatre were the best-equipped in the country. Contemporary prints show a straight-across forestage fronted by a curved orchestra-pit railing. Latrobe changed the stage apron to a semicircular front with a baffle masking the footlight trough. An eagle in the clouds hovered over a classical figure above the proscenium arch. Underneath the painting was inscribed, "For useful mirth or salutary woe." The auditorium was painted gray and the fronts of the boxes were gilded and decorated. Large corridors paved with marble, two greenrooms, gilded railings and festoons of beautiful auditorium draperies were some of the appointments mentioned in the press. European visitors praised the acoustics, orchestra and sightlines.

In 1816, the gas plant in Masonic Hall, a block from the theater, began supplying illumination for the Chestnut Street Theatre, making it the first gaslit American theater. Illuminating gas made strip-, foot- and border-lights possible for the first time. Open-flame gas tips were placed over a large pipe in the footlight trough and the area over the stage was lit with tapers prior to the raising of the curtain, the intensity controlled by means of a hand-operated gas valve. An advertisement in the *Aurora* of November 21, 1816, read: "The managers are happy to be the first to introduce the use of gas in lighting theatres in America and are flattered that its superior safety, brilliance and neatness will be satisfactorily experienced by the audience."

The Chestnut, sometimes advertised as the Philadelphia Theatre but usually referred to as the New Theatre (the Southwark being the Old Theatre), burned on Sunday, April 2, 1820. All that survived the tragic fire were a ship model, a mirror, a prompter's clock and the William Rush statues of Tragedy and Comedy, which fell into the street away from the burning building. Destroyed were the world-renowned English stage scenery, the lights, library, organ, machinery and musical instruments. Following the fire, the Chestnut company utilized the Walnut Street Theatre, which had opened in 1809. This arrangement, however, did not satisfy many Chestnut patrons, who considered the Walnut an unsafe circus. Meanwhile, plans were made for rebuilding the Chestnut on an enlarged lot of 92 by 150 feet.

William Strickland (1788–1854), an apprentice of Latrobe, was the architect for the replacement, which opened on December 2, 1822, again billed as the "New Theatre." Strickland contracted to build the theater for $45,000. Any confusion about the name ended when the theater began to be affectionately called "Old

The first Chestnut Street Theatre (on the right facing Congress Hall), at Sixth and Chestnut Streets, was constructed by the theatrical management firm of Reinagle & Wignell from the plan of a theater in Bath, England. Opened to the public on February 17, 1794, this, the most elegant and palatial theater in the United States, quickly became America's theatrical center. It was destroyed by fire on April 2, 1820. *(Athenaeum of Philadelphia.)*

The first Chestnut Street Theatre as altered in 1805 by English-born Benjamin Henry Latrobe (1764–1820), the first professional architect to work in America. The Chestnut was often referred to as the New Theatre (the Southwark was called the Old Theatre). *(Athenaeum of Philadelphia.)*

The third building of the first Chestnut Street Theatre was designed by architect William Strickland (1788–1854), a student of Latrobe's. It opened on December 2, 1822, and was demolished in 1855. The statues of Comedy and Tragedy, by America's first native-born sculptor of note, William Rush, had been saved from the 1820 fire and were reinstalled. They now survive in the collection of the Philadelphia Museum of Art. *(Athenaeum of Philadelphia.)*

Drury.'' Rush's salvaged statues were placed into niches in the exterior side wings. Between the two wings were five arches, each with an individual staircase. Tall, slender Corinthian columns supported a large pediment. Written sources from the period testify to the lavishness of the theater's interior.

The Chestnut was razed in 1855 in the belief that the forthcoming Academy of Music [1857] would deplete its patronage; the Academy, however, proved too large for dramatic productions—it engulfed the average play in deadening space. William Rush's statues found a third home when they were acquired by the Forrest Home for Actors; the Comedy and Tragedy figures were ultimately placed in the Philadelphia Museum of Art in 1985.

In 1795, a year after the first Chestnut began operations, the Art Pantheon (also called Rickett's Amphitheatre) opened directly across the street, making the intersection of Sixth and Chestnut Streets the center of Philadelphia's night life. Rickett's was a large circular tent of wood, 97 feet in diameter, with white 18-foot walls slanting upward to make a 50-foot-high conical roof. Although it was a circus, the handsomely porticoed building had a stage. Its seating capacity was between 600 and 700.

The largest fire Philadelphia had ever witnessed occurred on December 17, 1799, when Rickett's Amphitheatre and adjoining buildings went up in flames. The fire, which may have been caused by the incendiary set of hell in an ongoing production of *Don Juan*, was interpreted by many as a judgment of Providence. Conflagrations would continue to pose the greatest threat to

Philadelphia's theater buildings throughout the nineteenth century.

In 1809, the prestigious, spacious and elegant New Circus was opened by Pepin and Breschard at the northeast corner of Ninth and Walnut. Later a stage house was added and the structure was renamed the Olympic Theatre. Continuous rebuildings left only a portion of the original Ninth Street wall, and the entire theater has been altered repeatedly over the years.

In 1820 the Olympic became the Walnut Street Theatre. The acoustically poor dome was removed at this time by the management of the recently destroyed Chestnut Street Theatre. In 1822, the interior was restored to that of a circus and the name was changed back to the Olympic, although in 1827 it operated as the Philadelphia Theatre. In 1828, prominent Philadelphia architect John Haviland (1792–1852) redesigned the entire building. The interior was gutted, and a new foundation and interior walls added. Subsequent rebuildings (in 1903 by Willis G. Hale [1848–1907] and in 1920 by William H. Lee [1884–1971]) further altered and enlarged the theater. Today Haviland's restored facade masks a spartan auditorium and features four sets of glass doors flanked by Doric columns. The original entrance-doors now serve as exits; slender, freestanding gas-fired lighting fixtures have been once again placed between the columns; the second level consists of six 12-paned rectangular windows set within an arched frame, surmounted by a flat cornice with six inset balustrades, resembling the stonelike effect of the rest. The Walnut Street Theatre is the oldest theater in the United States in continuous operation, and is a National Historic Landmark.

The Walnut Street Theatre, Ninth and Walnut Streets, opened on February 2, 1809. This National Historic Landmark is the oldest theater in the United States in continuous operation. The restored facade is based on the original 1828 design by English-born and -trained John Haviland (1792–1852). Shown here is a late-nineteenth-century photograph of the Walnut. *(Athenaeum of Philadelphia.)*

Theater Buildings in Antebellum Philadelphia

The huge Washington Hall on Third Street, designed in 1809 by Robert Mills (1781–1855; the first American-born professional architect), opened in 1816 as the largest auditorium in the country, with a capacity of

6,000. The exterior featured a half-dome and portico over the main entrance. The interior had a balcony and lofty roof supported without interior columns. Fire took its toll in 1823, but the building was eventually restored to its original appearance. Washington Hall served as the meeting place of the Grand Lodge of Pennsylvania Masons from 1835 until 1855.

The Philadelphia Musical Fund Society (the country's oldest musical organization) was founded in 1820, and by 1824 had acquired an uncompleted church and rebuilt the structure into one of the country's most acoustically perfect concert halls. The hall was enlarged and altered in 1847 by architect Napoleon LeBrun (1821–1901). It was the favorite auditorium in the city until the erection of the Academy of Music. The present facade, which dates from an 1891 alteration, masks the building's current use as a condominium complex.

The Arch Street Theatre, at Sixth and Arch Streets, was designed by William Strickland and opened on October 1, 1828. When it was razed in 1936 it was the second oldest playhouse in the country. It was most prominent during the two decades after 1861, when it was managed by John and Louisa Drew, the maternal grandparents of the Barrymores, who appeared many times on the Arch stage. This photograph shows the crystal chandelier and the late-nineteenth-century Neo-Grec hand-painted dome, with eight flared panels in floral design.

In addition to the Chestnut and Walnut Street Theatres, Philadelphia's major theatrical venue was the Arch Street Theatre, which opened at Sixth and Arch Streets in 1828. Architect William Strickland designed a handsome marble facade consisting of a two-story-high portico supported by four pairs of Doric columns in the central portion and single columns at either end. These columns supported an entablature and balustrade of the Roman Doric order, which ran the full width of the building. Six broad steps led from the pavement to the central section of the portico. Behind the portico were two more stories comprising the full height of the theater. The center of the pediment featured a free-standing marble statue of Apollo by Nicholas Gevelot. This statue was removed during an 1863 remodeling and reinstalled at the third level of the new facade. The remodeling brought the upper stories out to the building line, eliminating the portico.

The spacious theater seated 1,911 in red-plush seats.

The interior design scheme of white and gold offset the crystal chandeliers. The glory of the auditorium was an elaborate hand-painted dome. There were two balconies, an orchestra and an orchestra circle. On either side of the orchestra pit was a box containing movable chairs. Four stage boxes on two levels completed the seating arrangement. The proscenium was 34½ feet wide and 22 feet high, the stage was 41 feet deep and 67 feet wide. There were ten dressing rooms.

The theater changed hands (and policy) many times. Its most auspicious era commenced in 1861, under the management of the Drews (grandparents of the Barrymores). Ethel, John and Lionel Barrymore grew up in Philadelphia, appearing many times on the stage of this fabled theater.

Six theaters were built in Philadelphia during the 1830s. Of particular architectural interest was the Chinese Museum. Opening on July 4, 1838, it was a two-story marble building with lofty ceilings. The "L"-shaped structure faced the east side of Ninth Street with an entrance and box office on Sansom Street. The stage was below the audience, the auditorium built in stadium style. In 1847, after the Chinese Museum collections were removed, the lower floor (originally Peale's Museum) was changed, along with a surrounding gallery, into a meeting-room/theater. Many public meetings of the day were held in the Chinese Museum. This was Philadelphia's first multitheater building: the lower floor held 3,000 people, and the upper, 5,000. A conflagration on July 5, 1854, destroyed the south side of Chestnut Street between Eighth and Ninth Streets, including the Chinese Museum.

Fire continued to destroy theaters in the 1850s, during which decade nine new venues opened. Although many of the theaters operating at this time had attractive decorations, they were for the most part uncomfortable. The seats were hard; the pit seats were usually long benches alternating with standing room. Ventilation was minimal, there was no heating and the threat of fires from candles and oil- and gas-lamps was ever-present. The major theaters, with British and European styles as prototypes, had curving balconies (usually divided into individual private boxes), making for poor sightlines. Polite society frowned upon women attending the theater: when they did, they were escorted by gentlemen and always sat in the first or second tier. The pit was for men and the gallery for poor folk. Blacks were allowed only in the galleries, and their ticket prices were double.

In 1857, the American Academy of Music opened at Broad and Locust Streets. Never used as a music school, the Academy is the world's oldest extant grand-opera house still in its original form. Designed by architects Napoleon LeBrun and Gustav Runge (1822–1900), the Academy was modeled after La Scala Opera House in Milan, modified to create seating in rows at each upper level.

LeBrun's desire to achieve acoustical perfection took him to Italy to study La Scala, and his creation is a jewel box of crystal, marble and red velvet. The main auditorium is done in cream and gold, with illuminated plaster reliefs of musical motifs serving as decorative facings for the balconies. Heroic, kneeling atlantes artistically support the roof above the proscenium box sections, and the whole is set off by the city's largest

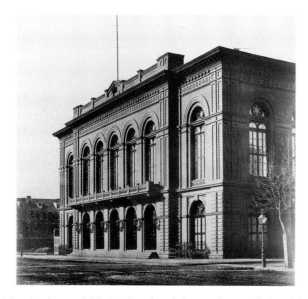

The Academy of Music, Broad and Locust Streets, designed by Napoleon LeBrun (1821–1901) and Gustav Runge (1822–1900), is one of the oldest auditoriums in the United States still in use for its original purposes, and the oldest grand opera house standing in its original form in the world. A Registered National Historic Landmark, the Academy is the resident home of the renowned Philadelphia Orchestra and the Philadelphia Opera Company. *(Athenaeum of Philadelphia.)*

crystal chandelier. This great light fixture contains hidden spotlights that highlight the dome and the surrounding frescoes by Karl Heinrich Schmolze (1823–1861) depicting Poetry, Music, Dance, Comedy and Tragedy. A medallion visage of Mozart dominates the center of the auditorium-height proscenium arch. The four walls were purposely left exposed to the elements for a year before the roof went on so that the walls could dry perfectly. Large quantities of cows' hair went into the mortar to absorb sound.

There are five levels of seating, an orchestra floor called The Parquet, a raised Parquet Circle and Balcony, Family Circle and Amphitheatre levels. Each subsequent horizontal has an increased angle of sight in addition to being further recessed, making the highest point precipitous. There are 26 parquet boxes, an equal number of balcony boxes, and six large proscenium boxes. Broad promenades completely encircle each level—including the parquet and the horseshoe balconies—thereby insulating the auditorium with a double wall. The balcony promenade accesses a large ballroom built atop the entrance lobbies. This cove-lit room, with its crystal chandeliers and mirrored doors and walls, was modeled after the Great Hall of Versailles, and in turn inspired the lobbies of many twentieth-century eclectic movie palace lobbies throughout the country.

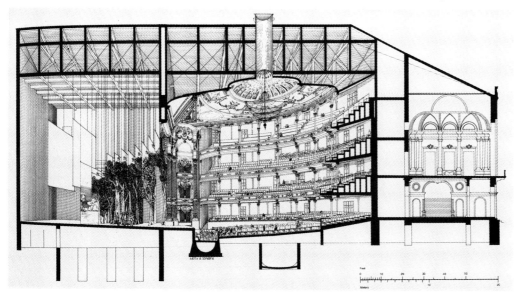

This longitudinal perspective shows the original arrangement of the Academy of Music for opera productions. *(© The George C. Izenour Archive.)*

This drawing shows the twentieth-century remodeling of the Academy of Music that placed seating over the original orchestra pit and created an orchestra shell on the stage. *(© The George C. Izenour Archive.)*

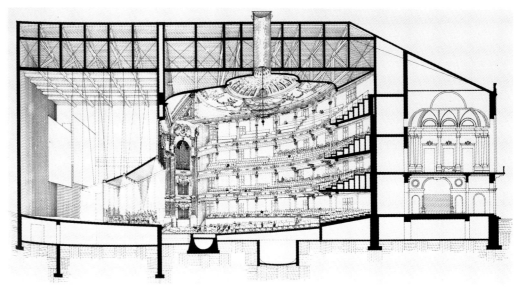

Victorian Theater Buildings

The new Chestnut Street Theatre, between 12th and 13th Streets, opened on January 26, 1863. This house filled the need for another large legitimate theater that followed the hasty demolition of "Old Drury" in 1855. It took only a few months to erect the theater, creating the spiteful rumor that the structure was unsafe: as a consequence the house was only about one-third filled on opening night. The four-story facade resembled a nineteenth-century office building. A cast-iron awning extended to the curb line, and when exterior fire escapes were mandated, the final staircase was cut through the awning. Later, this exterior became an aesthetic concern to the Chestnut Street Businessmen's Association because the nineteenth-century building line protruded five feet further than its neighbors'.

The Chestnut Street Theatre, 1211–15 Chestnut Street, designed by architect John Crump (1827–1892), opened in 1863. This early-twentieth-century photo shows how the introduction of electric signs and the newly mandated fire escapes affected the stately Victorian facade of the theater.

The interior was altered on several occasions. Early floor plans show three balconies. The seating in the top balcony or fourth level was seven rows of long benches on a steep incline. The box seats had a bowl design similar to that of the later Chestnut Street Opera House. A large dome, painted in a floral design, was the main decoration in an otherwise drab interior. In 1876, following the installation of a steam-powered fan, the theater announced that it was the coolest playhouse in Philadelphia. Initial seating capacity was listed at 2,100; the original architect, John Crump (1827–1892), also designed the Colosseum Cyclorama building at Broad and Locust in 1876. Architect John D. Allen (fl. 1890–1923) did alterations to the Chestnut in 1891, 1898 and 1901.

Early in the twentieth century, when the theater fell on hard times, it opened and closed so many times that it

was referred to as "The Morgue." When demolition plans were announced in 1917, the *Philadelphia Public Ledger* commented, "It will be a sentimental rather than an architectural loss . . . it is nothing more than an eyesore."

Horticultural Hall, referred to as the most beautiful public assembly room in the city, opened (with a flower show, appropriately) on South Broad Street in 1867. Elaborate interior ornamentation and a fanciful Florentine facade enhanced the elegance of the location. In 1881, the cornice on the Hall's roof was ignited by a fire in a church just to the south. The hall was completely destroyed, but the Academy of Music, its neighbor to the north, was spared. Horticultural Hall was rebuilt and was again destroyed by fire in 1893 (the Academy was saved once again). A third building lasted until 1918, when it was replaced by the Sam S. Shubert Memorial Theatre. The Hall's sweeping pink Tennessee-marble divided staircase was saved and reused as the first balcony approach in the new theater. The backstage wall of the Shubert is also taken from the predecessor building.

The Trocadero, originally known as the Arch Street Opera House (and later operated under eleven different other names), is on the National Register of Historic Places, along with the Walnut and the Academy of Music. Designed by Edwin F. Durang (1829–1911), the theater opened in August 1870. The Trocadero underwent numerous design changes after several fires in the first two decades of its existence. The auditorium was also redesigned in 1892, 1894 and 1896 by architect George Plowman (fl. 1876–1903). Initial seating capacities varied from 900 to 1,000, depending on how many people could be squeezed onto the gallery benches.

This building, now known familiarly as the Troc, is the only nineteenth-century Victorian popular theater left intact in the United States. The restored theater, which reopened in 1979, constitutes a welcome addition to the city's depleted roster of medium-sized concert venues. As such, the Philadelphia Opera Company has

The Trocadero Theatre, Tenth and Arch Streets, opened on August 20, 1870, as the Arch Street Opera House. Three fires and twelve name or management changes later, this house was placed on the National Register of Historic Places. The original architect was Edwin F. Durang (1829–1911); alterations were supervised by George Plowman in the 1890s. The "Troc" is the only intact nineteenth-century Victorian popular theater in the United States. *(Glazer Collection; photo by George E. Thomas.)*

used the theater, although hampered by the "hemp house" backstage and by the lack of wing space. The original 50-foot stage depth had been reduced to 30 feet by dressing rooms built across the back.

The 3½-story 1870 brick building was painted to imitate marble. The entrance was through a 16-foot areaway flanked by retail stores. The frescoed entrance hall was forty feet long and hung with paintings. The three-level auditorium was frescoed and the theater was primarily illuminated by a gas reflector that hung from the dome. The second theater, erected after an 1872 fire, was designed in an Italianate style after Edwin F. Durang's original plans. George Plowman's numerous subsequent alterations removed the stores to create new entranceways in the auditorium and balconies. The present facade consists of three arched entrances with stained glass in the upper portions. Above are three two-story-high Second Empire window frames in white, constrasting with the red brickwork. The present lobby includes doors and woodwork from the defunct Erlanger Theatre and a Baroque plaster indirect-illumination chandelier from the Burgundy Ballroom of the Bellevue Stratford Hotel. The auditorium, painted creamy yellow with orange, blue and gilt trim, retains its original mirrored walls (once hidden behind mahogany paneling) as well as a mirrored orchestra-pit railing.

The ceiling preserves Victorian stencilings of floral garlands and classical figures. Cast-iron railings in a filigree design face the balcony and the gallery. A plaster double-garland design frames the proscenium. Restoration has revealed egg-and-dart moldings, classical cornices, plaster lions flanking the stage, cast-iron ornamental columns, the original asbestos curtain and the original gallery benches.

Dumont's Theatre, originally called the American Museum, Menagerie and Theatre, opened at Ninth and Arch Streets in 1870. It was a four-story Victorian structure with a mansard roof, ornamented dormers and a series of porthole windows with iron crestings at the roof level. The first three floors had a smooth concrete finish pierced by a two-story recessed arch at the center of the Arch Street facade.

When Dumont took over with his minstrel company in 1911, the building was painted a buff color and an angled canopy with electric titles was placed at the entrance. The theater burned in 1929.

Nineteen theaters in all were destroyed by fire between 1799 and 1871, more than one-third of the total constructed. Though there was no loss of life among theatergoers, an actor at the Chestnut Street National Theatre, Rensselaer Albert Shepard, was caught in collapsing ruins and burned to death in 1854.

In 1873 the Olympic Theatre opened at 1226 Market Street, in the converted shell of the 1856 National Hall. With a stage modeled after that of the Academy of Music, the new theater billed itself as the "Largest & Handsomest in the City." Its short-lived grandeur was ended by a fire in 1874 that leveled the theater.

In 1876 Philadelphia became the "Centennial City," celebrating the nation's 100th birthday with a hugely successful international exposition attracting ten million people. The Kiralfy brothers, who specialized in spectacular productions, decided to build a lavish temporary theater in the center of town to house performances for the duration of the exposition. At their behest, architect Frank H. Loenholdt created a fantastic confection resembling the fairground's Main Building in miniature. Municipal building regulations required that brick be used rather than wood, so the structure became a permanent one.

Fourteen arches fronted the Broad Street facade, with light fixtures suspended from eight recessed

Dumont's Theatre, Ninth and Arch Streets, opened in 1870 as the American Museum. Alterations completed in 1892 by architect George Plowman (fl. 1876–1903) are represented in this 1914 photo. The theater burned in 1929. (*Philadelphia City Archives.*)

The Broad Street Theatre, Broad and Locust Streets, designed by architect Frank H. Loenholdt, opened in 1876 and was demolished in 1937. This eclectic, gaudy, colorful confection seemed out of place on staid Broad Street. The domes were painted with a variety of bold primary colors and were later highlighted with hundreds of electric light bulbs. Originally designed to attract visitors to the Centennial Exposition of 1876, the Broad Street hosted huge musicals on its large stage. By the twentieth century, after numerous architectural alterations, a much-subdued facade fronted one of the city's leading legitimate playhouses.

arcades. The center four accessed a broad landing that served as an entrance to the orchestra floor. Two large polychromatic domes surmounted the thrust sections, complemented by smaller domes at each end of the building. Spires, spirals and embryonic minarets, in addition to garish colorations in the trim and fanlights,

In this 1937 pre-demolition photograph, the Broad Street Theatre lobby still retained a portion of its original Moorish design.

enhanced a design that could best be termed Broad Street Moorish.

The theater was opened as Kiralfy's Alhambra Palace, and the name was well deserved. Dancing girls, magnificent costuming and scenery, real fawns, 40 hunting dogs and even an elephant were part of glittering productions. Even with so much to offer, however, attendance was sparse. A financially beleaguered Kiralfy sold the theater at a fraction of its cost, and it ultimately became the Broad Street Theatre. Ironically, the Broad Street became the preferred playhouse of Philadelphia society prior to its demolition in 1937—most probably because of its location across Broad from the Academy of Music.

A Bijou Theatre opened at 253 North Eighth Street in 1877, the first of ten theaters in the city to bear that name. Twelve years later, another theater, called Keith's Bijou, opened at the southern end of the same block. In 1884, the first Bijou adopted its third and final name, Forepaugh's. The theater remained an important legitimate and repertory house until the neighborhood deteriorated in the early twentieth century.

Designed by the Wilson Brothers, Forepaugh's three-story brick Victorian facade had two upper-story iron balconies extending over Eighth Street. In the 1930s the brick was painted red, yellow and bright green. The auditorium was shallow, with two balconies supported from below by eight cast-iron poles—creating the usual sightline problems. The pitch of the gallery was so steep that it was difficult to negotiate. The theater was redecorated several times, but the original ceiling with murals of diaphanously clad females flitting among palm trees was still intact when the structure was demolished in 1960.

The next major theater was the Chestnut Street Opera House, one of the most important legitimate theaters of the 1880s owing to its location and large (1,656) capacity. The 1913 alterations by architects Bissell & Sinkler required a setback of five feet to conform to city law. The new facade had a severe classical look. Three 24-foot arches supported a frieze engraved with the theater name. Four pairs of Corinthian columns and two plain pilasters framed six double-corniced Italianate double windows. A rooftop balustrade completed a handsome picture. 1929 alterations by architect Herbert Krapp (1887–1973) straightened the horseshoe balconies, removed the stage apron and faced the garish, fishbowl-shaped box seats toward the stage. Twenty dressing rooms made the theater adequate for large productions. When the theater was torn down in 1940, it marked the first time in almost 150 years that Chestnut Street had no legitimate theater.

Many venues of this era, such as the Palm Theatre (1887; altered 1919) at Frankford and Norris, offered a range of programs, including stock drama and vaudeville. Featuring a massive five-story Victorian brick facade, the Palm exemplified the material grandeur of the Gilded Age; nonetheless it fell into twentieth-century disuse, suffered a transition to a used-furniture store in the 1950s, and was finally demolished in 1970, after years of vacancy and fires.

The Palm Theatre, Frankford Avenue and Norris Street, was originally built in 1887 with alterations in 1919 by architect Reuben Beard (fl. 1915–1936). This large Victorian vaudeville theater was sold to a used-furniture dealer for $1,000 in 1954. Plagued with repeated fires, the theater was demolished in 1970.

The Grand Opera House—located at Broad and Montgomery, miles from the theater district—opened in 1888 as the home of the National Opera Company, initiating a brief phase of Philadelphia's having two opera houses, which would last only until 1892. Designed by George Plowman for the Betz Brewing Company, the Grand Opera House underwent numerous alterations, including those by Thomas Lamb in 1913 and Hoffman & Henon in 1923. The large orchestra floor had 40 rows, allowing a capacity of from 3,000 to 4,000. Later, the Grand Opera House became the Nixon Grand and was one of the two major vaudeville houses in the city.

The fourth-largest theater ever erected in Philadelphia, the Grand Opera House maintained its original facade, resembling that of a Betz brewery, throughout its 53-year duration. Twenty-nine windows fronted the office-building section of the theater. The stage house was 60 feet deep and 150 feet wide, and towered one and a half stories higher than the auditorium section. Interior photos taken just before demolition show a Moorish design, smothered in fringed and tasseled draperies. After several major fires, the building was demolished in 1940.

Variety shows became respectable with the appearance on the local scene of Benjamin Franklin Keith, whose name appeared bulbed, painted or engraved in front of vaudeville houses for decades. His first in Philadelphia was a small, ornate theater called Keith's Bijou. The 1,200-seat theater opened on November 4, 1889 at the northeast corner of Eighth and Race Streets. Before Keith's, a family man would not consider taking his wife or children to a variety theater, but the Bijou was different. It was advertised as "the Drawing Room Theatre of Philadelphia—High Class, Refined Entertainment."

The Bijou's management maintained strict standards of decorum backstage as well as at the front of the house (the sidewalk in front of the Bijou was constantly scrubbed clean). An innovation was their introduction of "continuous performances." The ticket-price scale was 25¢ for orchestra-, 20¢ for balcony- and 10¢ for gallery-seating.

The 200 block of North Eighth Street was a rialto, the home to no less than 21 theaters over the years. Urban planners in charge of designing the nearby Delaware River Bridge approach confidently predicted that this section would be a bustling business district once the bridge opened. They were mistaken: the area eventually became a tenderloin of flophouses, soup kitchens and tawdry saloons. The doomed theater sank gradually from vaudeville to burlesque. Similarly, the Park Theatre, which opened as a legitimate theater the same year, succumbed to the decline of North Broad Street and became a burlesque house as early as 1911. The early 1890s saw the construction of a few more grand theaters of the old style (such as the People's [1890], Empire [1891] and Gayety [1892]).

The Park Theatre, Broad Street and Fairmount Avenue, designed by architect John B. McElfatrick (1828–1906), opened on September 16, 1889, in what was rapidly becoming a fashionable theater district. During the 1968 demolition of this variety house, an original second balcony, intact with Victorian stencilings, plaster reliefs and light fixtures, was discovered above a later dropped ceiling.

The People's Theatre, 2649 Kensington Avenue (architect: George Plowman), opened on August 23, 1890, with a repertory stock policy. In 1928, the interior was gutted and the lavish Kent Theatre was built within the original walls. Hoffman & Henon were the architects who designed a modern facade and innovative stadium seating in the auditorium. The Frankford Elevated Line, completed in 1922, obliterated the upper exterior portions of both theaters.

The Empire Theatre, Broad and Locust Streets, was designed by architect Willis G. Hale (1848–1907) and opened in 1891. This elaborate work may have been Philadelphia's only theater built in the Queen Anne style. Before it was replaced by the Walton Hotel (also designed by Hale) in 1898, this theater and the adjacent Broad Street Theatre presented a fantastic architectural contrast to the staid Academy of Music, directly across Broad Street.

This 1926 photo shows the ornate detailing of the entrance to the People's Theatre prior to its alteration by Hoffman & Henon.

The Gayety Theatre, 237 North Eighth Street (architects: Rowe & Dagit), opened in 1892. The cross-section shown depicts the lavish Victorian detail that the architects designed. This was the largest theater on what became known as Philadelphia's theatrical rialto. North Eighth Street between Race and Vine Streets was home to at least 21 theaters at the turn of the century. When the Gayety was torn down in 1953, its entranceway pillars remained as the city's most ornate approach to a parking lot. (*Dagit Collection, Athenaeum of Philadelphia.*)

The Beginnings of the Film Era

The future of public entertainment in Philadelphia was foreshadowed by an unusual exhibition at Keith's Bijou in 1895. On Christmas Day of that year the first projected motion picture with flexible film ever shown in Philadelphia appeared there. The motion-picture machine used was called the Eidoscope, the invention of Woodville Latham. This exhibition was probably the first of its kind in the world. The first public demonstration in Paris of the Lumière machine was on December 28, 1895.

In 1896 the Bijou featured Lumière's Cinematograph, and afterwards motion pictures were always included on the bill. Thus, only seven years after its opening, the Bijou Theatre was exhibiting films similar to those of the forthcoming silent-screen era to amazed audiences. The Bijou had a brief period of preeminence, but its film innovations mainly presaged the coming movie-palace era—both in its excesses and in its artistic triumphs. Subsequent decades saw explosive growth in motion-picture buildings, from the modest offerings of temporary installations such as Lubin's Cineograph and storefront nickelodeons to the palatial movie palaces of the golden age of Hollywood.

By 1900 box seats did not encroach onto projecting stage aprons and most stage areas had retreated behind a proscenium frame. Horseshoe seating plans, with the resultant impaired sightlines, became things of the past. The introduction of steel cantilever trusses eliminated the forests of poles, and single deep balconies gradually did away with galleries. Theaters became wider but lost the sensation of great open space that had been possible with numerous and shallow balconies. To create large seating capacities, the single great balcony came closer to the stage and, at the top, led to the back wall of the theater over the lobbies. A few theaters with galleries were built during the first decade of the twentieth century, but this type of construction was not to return except in the case of concert halls. A corollary reversal

Lubin's Cineograph was a popular feature on the midway of the National Export Exposition held in Fairmount Park in 1898. "Cineograph" was the trade name for a projector marketed by film pioneer Siegmund Lubin (c. 1851–1923), who, for a time, made Philadelphia an important motion-picture production center. (*Free Library of Philadelphia.*)

of taste in seating was the newfound preference for orchestra seating, now that women had emerged from the hidden depths and shelter of the enclosed tiers of private boxes. Galleries that remained in the older theaters now catered to the clientele who had previously occupied the pit, renamed with the more elegant-sounding parquet or orchestra designation. Everyone, it seems, wanted to sit downstairs or in the first few rows of the upstairs, also renamed the mezzanine.

Introduction to the Plates

"The illusion that times that were are better than those that are, has, probably, pervaded all ages."
—Horace Greeley

THE theaters of my youth were no doubt already faded with age when I first saw them. I nevertheless remain transfigured by my memories of the showiness and opulence of those imaginative buildings. In retrospect, the majority of Philadelphia's theaters seem simple and restrained—decoratively elegant, with classical tendencies. A comparison of Philadelphia's theater palaces with those of Chicago, New York or San Francisco demonstrates in most cases a Philadelphian restraint and simplicity of design. The exceptions, however, were notable, as the pictorial coverage to follow affirms.

The movie palace was perhaps the most important new type of building introduced in the twentieth century. Its advent marked the first time in architectural history that ornate and costly structures were conceived and executed primarily for the service of the common man. In commenting on the opening of the Uptown Theatre, architect Louis Magaziner said, "It may be conceded that the palace of autocracy is the playhouse of democracy. Where royalty deemed it as its own particularly ordained right to revel in the created beauty of its artists and craftsmen, democracy is now privileged to enjoy such creations for its hours of leisure." Extravagantly decorated theaters were often built in the poorest neighborhoods, where, along with church buildings, they provided much-needed architectural landmarks. The beginning of the twentieth century saw a quantitative surge in theater construction. Of the more than 800 theaters constructed in Philadelphia, 430 were built between 1900 and 1932. As the leisure time of an increasingly affluent working class grew, so did the demand for theaters. Though moviegoing was certainly not inhibited by the advent of the Great Depression, the economic catastrophes of that era devastated theater building. By the end of World War II, television and the growth of the suburbs spelled doom for many existing theaters and slowed the construction of new ones. The following pages depict the mostly vanished evidences of the heritage of Philadelphia's golden age of theater buildings.

—IRVIN R. GLAZER

Keith's Theatre

Opposite, top: Keith's Theatre, also known as Chestnut Street Keith's, 1116 Chestnut Street, was designed by architect Albert E. Westover (fl. 1899–1919), and opened on November 10, 1902, as Philadelphia's first "million-dollar" theater. The second of Keith's Philadelphia vaudeville houses, it had daily matinee and evening "star" performances. A city block in length, Keith's Theatre had numerous lobbies with extravagant French Renaissance fittings. In 1949 the lavish interior was completely gutted to create a motion picture house, which survived until 1971. Shown is a portion of the Crystal lobby, the third entranceway from Chestnut Street.

Opposite, bottom: The Grand Entrance Hall of Keith's, including marble staircases, ornate iron railings and a crystal chandelier, was open to the street. The freestanding box office is visible at the center of this photo.

Above: At the time of this 1917 photo Keith's was the most important local theater presenting vaudeville, the prime popular entertainment of the day. Shown are the main-floor usherettes in Keith's Music Salon.

The Lyric and Adelphi Theatres

Above: The Lyric and Adelphi Theatres (1905 and 1907, respectively), Broad and Cherry Streets, were designed by architect James H. Windrim (1840–1919), whose most prominent commission, the Masonic Temple, was located one block to the south. Sharing a common facade, these were Philadelphia's first twin theaters. The wider and shallower Lyric auditorium had a larger stage and greater seating capacity than its "twin." Both were torn down in 1937, by which time Broad Street north of City Hall was no longer a fashionable theater district. Among the theatrical cognoscenti, these theaters were referred to as the "Cherry Street Sisters." *(Dillon Collection, Athenaeum of Philadelphia.)*

Below: Broad Street, facing south from Race, c. 1920. At the left in this photo are the Lyric and Adelphi Theatres, in the center is Philadelphia's City Hall and to the right is the Pennsylvania Academy of the Fine Arts.

The Palace Theatre

Above: The Palace Theatre, 1214 Market Street, was built in 1908 for film pioneer Siegmund Lubin as his largest center-city outlet. In 1921, architects Hoffman & Henon transformed the spartan lobby into this marble and brass creation.

Below: The Palace Theatre was an example of what became known as "bowling alley" architecture, with a block-length auditorium. With exits at both ends only, no side alleys were necessary. This economy feature eliminated the need for additional expensive Market and Chestnut Street frontage. A full stage was used for both vaudeville and movies until the 1921 alteration (pictured) placed the components of a large pipe organ behind the screen.

The Metropolitan Opera House

Opposite, top: The Metropolitan Opera House, Broad and Poplar Streets, opened in 1908. The architect was William H. McElfatrick (1854–1922). Oscar Hammerstein, Sr., envisioned building a chain of major opera houses throughout the country to challenge the supremacy of New York's Metropolitan Opera. This venue on North Broad Street, originally called the Philadelphia Opera House, was the second and final building of the impresario's ambitious plan. The 240-foot main facade, shown here under construction, was the widest of any theater constructed in Philadelphia. Similar entrances are on the parallel Carlisle Street; the parquet boxes were accessed from Poplar Street, intersecting at the right.

Opposite, bottom: The Metropolitan Opera House, November 17, 1908—opening night. The cast-iron Broad Street marquee, shown here, was the largest of four. There were thirteen separate entrances on this side of the building, each with two or three doors. Hammerstein had learned about circulation spaces from the poor design of his first opera house, New York's Manhattan.

Left, top: The Metropolitan had 36 proscenium boxes, with the second level continuing into a thrust entresol containing 28 additional boxes—most of which featured separate rear drawing-rooms. Three additional levels of gallery-height boxes are shown: together with the parquet circle boxes they produced a combined total of 88 private boxes. Seats on the parquet floor all had individual armrests. In 1908 this was the largest opera house in the world, with a total capacity of 3,482.

Left, bottom: By the time of this 1928 photograph, North Broad Street was no longer an opera and legitimate-theater center, and the interior of the Metropolitan had been adapted for moving pictures. The entresol housed a projection booth, and the third and fourth levels of the proscenium boxes and their drawing rooms were transformed into chambers for the city's largest theater organ—the console mounted on a disappearing lift mechanism. The Grand Opera House, further north on Broad Street, had already turned to a similar vaudeville/movie policy. Both ventures were short-lived: the Grand was demolished in 1940; the Met remains, deteriorated, but essentially intact.

The William Penn Theatre

Opposite, top: The William Penn Theatre, 4063 Lancaster Avenue, designed by architects Carl Berger (1873–1947) and Mathew Schmid & Son, opened in 1909 as West Philadelphia's leading vaudeville theater, with a 40-foot-deep stage. Atop the theater was a 137-foot-high tower with a flashing beacon light. The mural by Adolph Frie, above the proscenium, depicts William Penn's treaty with the Indians.

The Victoria Theatre

Opposite, bottom: The Victoria Theatre, 913 Market Street (architects: Stearns & Castor), opened in 1909. This theater was a Siegmund Lubin operation, featuring his Philadelphia-based studio's motion pictures as well as vaudeville. This late-1940s photo shows how the monumental triumphal-arch facade (nearly six stories high) dominated this block in the heart of the Market Street retail district.

The Hill Theatre

Above: The Hill Theatre, 8320 Germantown Avenue, was altered in 1936 by the prolific theater architect William H. Lee (1884–1971). Opened as the Belvedere in 1916, the Hill featured a Georgian Revival exterior that complemented the interior, which was decorated to resemble a dignified old mansion from the early days of the nation. This 1931 photograph was taken prior to Lee's complete facade masking.

The Forrest Theatre

Opposite, top: The Forrest Theatre, Broad and Sansom Streets, was designed by architects Marshall & Fox, with Amos W. Barnes (1867–1953). The only legitimate theater in Philadelphia with a below-street-level orchestra floor, it had auditorium-length raised loge sections that could be closed to make the house more "intimate." A large (49 feet deep by 90 feet wide) stage made this the leading musical-comedy theater during its brief (1907–1927) existence.

Opposite, bottom: Architect Benjamin Marshall (1874–1945) said, at the opening of the Forrest Theatre, "We no doubt could have seated at least fifty percent more customers in the theatre . . . Why not give your patrons more [space] than the law requires? You will never regret it." The two-story front of the "L"-shaped theater was not economical, however, in the midst of the high-rise area of South Broad Street. The Fidelity Trust Building, by architects Simon & Simon, replaced the Forrest in 1927.

The Nixon Theatre

Above: The Nixon Theatre, 28 South 52nd Street, was the work of architect John D. Allen (fl. 1890–1923). Opened on November 21, 1910, the Nixon boasted a marble and crystal interior—and replaced a tent in which a ten-cent charge bought the customer five vaudeville acts. Among the distinguishing features of the Nixon: a separate side-street box office for balcony patrons and its own power plant. Demolition occurred in 1984.

MAY 1ST 1911.
RESPECTFULLY DEDICATED TO THE PATRONS OF THE GERMANTOWN THEATRE

Germantown Theatre
ANNIVERSARY MARCH

PIANO SOLO BY

JOHN B. HARTRANFT

PHILA, PA.
PUB. BY GEO. F. & W. STUEMPFIG.

Copyright by Geo F AND W. Stuempfig

The Germantown Theatre

Above: The Germantown Theatre, 5508 Germantown Avenue (architects: Druckenmiller & Stackhouse), was dubbed "The Pride of Germantown." This stage, stock and screen operation was one year old when this piano solo was composed. Music publishers Geo. F. & W. Stuempfig were the owners of the theater. The massive facade arch was duplicated in the interior proscenium arch. *(Atwater Kent Museum.)*

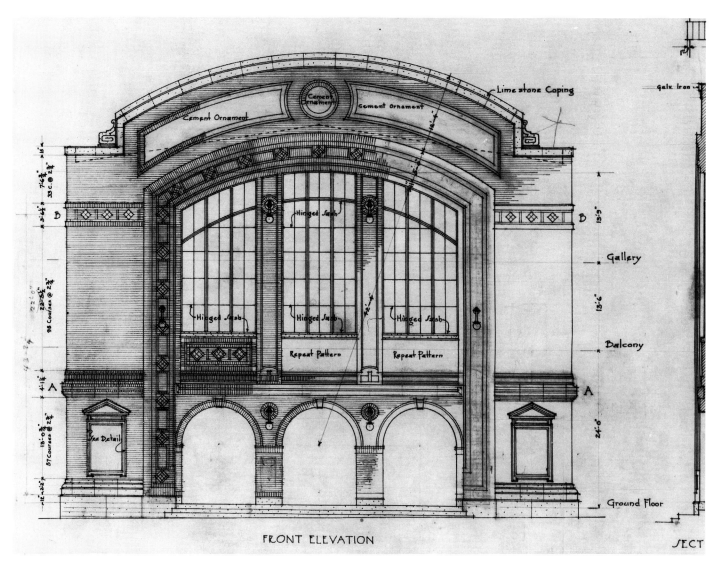

FRONT ELEVATION

The Allegheny Theatre

Above: The Allegheny Theatre, 3141 Frankford Avenue, was designed by architects Magaziner & Potter. This 1912 architectural drawing depicts the original front elevation. *(Magaziner Collection, Athenaeum of Philadelphia.)*

Right: This 1945 photo shows the Allegheny's facade as it was ultimately executed. This Keith vaudeville house never had a marquee.

Overleaf: This interior photo reveals that lavish and elegantly appointed theaters were not restricted to downtown addresses. The Allegheny, in the heart of Kensington's factory district, installed a Philadelphia first: the large stage had an orchestra elevator arrangement consisting of eight platform lifts that could be raised or lowered individually or in combination.

The Orpheum Theatre

Above: The Orpheum Theatre, 42 West Chelten Avenue, was a Beaux-Arts delight from the hands of architect John D. Allen, with Sauer & Hahn. The overwhelming red plush Orpheum opened in May 1912 with Keith vaudeville. The exterior archways had ascending seashell-design ceilings illuminated by floor lights, with the entire facade lighted by reflector-floods across the marquee.

The Broadway Theatre

Opposite, top: The Broadway Theatre, 2042 South Broad Street (architect: Albert E. Westover), was South Philadelphia's top vaudeville location. But the opera-loving Italian neighborhood also supported many bookings of traveling opera companies.

The Regent Theatre

Opposite, bottom: The Regent Theatre, 1632 Market Street, was designed by architect W. Burney in 1913. After five name changes, this silent-, art- and finally porno-film location met the wrecker's ball in 1980. The block, now primarily occupied by the Liberty Place Complex, was at one time home to the highest concentration of operating theaters in the city: the Center, Studio, Milgram, Fox, Stage Door, Regency, Duke and Duchess.

The Stanton Theatre

Above: The Stanton Theatre, 16th and Market Streets, was the work of the W. H. Hoffman Company, architects. On April 25, 1914, Stanley Mastbaum, president of the Stanley Company, memorialized himself when he opened this theater as the "Stanley." The theater engaged a symphony orchestra to accompany the silent pictures, and between showings concert artists performed on its stage. An unfortunate feature of the theater was a precipitous balcony that necessitated the installation of Philadelphia's only theater escalator in the 1940s.

[*17*]

The Crosskeys Theatre

Above: The Crosskeys Theatre, 5931 Market Street, was designed by architects Hoffman & Henon. The largest of three theaters in the half block between 59th and Salford, this charming vaudeville playhouse opened on December 28, 1914, on the former site of a tavern and a hotel bearing the same name.

Opposite, top: The elegant promenade at the rear of the orchestra section reflects the spaciousness of the Crosskeys Theatre.

Opposite, bottom: This 1914 interior photograph of the Crosskeys Theatre shows a portion of the fire curtain, painted to resemble the main curtain in the Paris Opera House.

The Arcadia Theatre

Opposite, top: The Arcadia Theatre, 1529 Chestnut Street (architects: Henon & Boyle), opened in 1915 as a first-run silent-picture theater. The interior lobby shown had polished brown-marble columns and walls. Reflecting the period is the rack at the left, containing printed programs of the current features and coming attractions.

Opposite, bottom: A restrained French Renaissance style remained in the Arcadia until its conversion to a fast-food restaurant in 1978. Note the wall-mounted fans and the set of exit doors under the screen. Adjacent to the right exit is the console of the theater organ used to accompany the films. The two organ chambers shown are tastefully disguised with draperies, valances and green ferns. A third, "echo," organ chamber was at the entrance end of the auditorium.

The Lincoln Theatre

Above: The Lincoln Theatre, Broad and Lombard Streets, opened as a "colored" legitimate theater in 1919 featuring the Lafayette Players, a Harlem repertory group. Eighteen box seats on three levels flanked what became a vaudeville, moving-picture and legitimate house. This photo was taken in 1932. *(Philadelphia City Archives.)*

The Eureka Theatre

Above: The Eureka Theatre, 40th and Market Streets, was designed by architects Stearns & Castor. The full terra-cotta ornamentation of this 1913 theater could be best viewed from the window of a passing Market Street elevated train or from the 40th Street Station platform.

The Samuel S. Shubert Memorial Theatre

Opposite, top: The Samuel S. Shubert Memorial Theatre, 250 South Broad Street, was designed by Herbert J. Krapp (1887–1973). From its 1918 opening, the Shubert was one of the city's leading legitimate theaters. Acquired by the University of the Arts, the Shubert underwent a splendid multimillion-dollar restoration that was completed in 1987 (architect: Rafael Villamil). On December 11, 1991, the Shubert was renamed The Merriam Theatre with ceremonies featuring a symphony orchestra performing in Philadelphia's largest orchestra pit.

Opposite, bottom: A longitudinal section of the Samuel S. Shubert Memorial Theatre, from *Architecture and Building* magazine, January 1918.

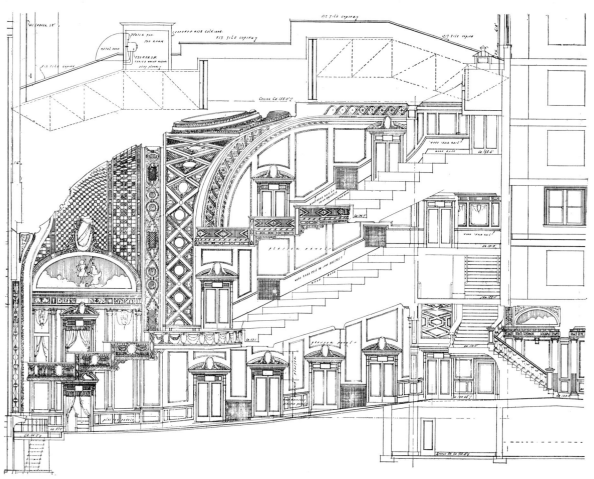

The Royal Theatre

Opposite, top: The Royal Theatre, 1524 South Street, designed by architect Frank E. Hahn (1879–1962), opened in 1920. Hahn's Neo-Georgian facade is at odds with the theater's 1925 Art Deco interior, designed by William H. Lee. Opened as "America's Finest Colored Photoplay House," the small stage also hosted many prominent black stars. The Royal's staff became the nucleus of the Negro Motion Picture Operators Union. *(Glazer Collection; photo by George E. Thomas.)*

Opposite, bottom: This photo, taken in the 1970s, shows the interior of the closed Royal Theatre. *(Glazer Collection; photo by George E. Thomas.)*

The Ambassador Theatre

Above: The Ambassador Theatre, 5542 Baltimore Avenue, opened in 1921, was one of the handsomest of the West Philadelphia neighborhood theaters. This 1956 picture was taken after the removal of the ten-foot-high building-width electric sign mounted on the roof.

The Stanley Theatre

Opposite, top: The Stanley Theatre, 19th and Market Streets (architects: Hoffman & Henon), was the second theater named after Stanley Mastbaum. When this house opened in 1921, the first Stanley Theatre became the Stanton. The new president of the Stanley Company, Jules Mastbaum, made the theater into a musical center as well as a moving-picture theater.

Opposite, bottom left: The world's greatest concert and operatic stars played the Stanley, where the pit orchestra was considered second only to the Philadelphia Orchestra (which also appeared on this stage). The design "was pure Adam up to the footlights; onstage was a Market Street version of Scheherazade's boudoir," wrote historian Ben M. Hall in *The Best Remaining Seats* (1961), the definitive history of the theater palace era.

Opposite, bottom right: Stanley Theatre program cover, December 8, 1924.

The Aldine Theatre

Above: The Aldine Theatre, 19th and Chestnut Streets, designed by architects William Steele & Sons. Rust-colored tapestry brick trimmed with white terra-cotta dignify this corner location. The interior was in lavish Empire style. The Aldine's opening nights became an institution in the theatrical life of the city's social set. But by 1967, the Aldine had deteriorated to the point that the *Philadelphia Evening Bulletin* dubbed the theater "the only flophouse in America with Cinemascope."

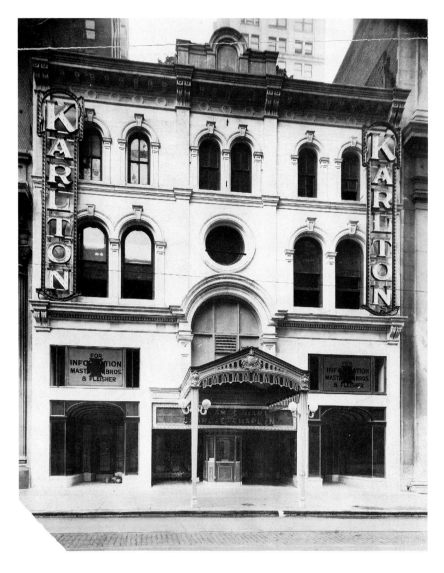

The Karlton Theatre

Left, top: The Karlton Theatre, 1412 Chestnut Street, opened in 1921, was designed by architects Hoffman & Henon. When the Midtown Theatre opened at this location in 1954, the limestone and marble facade shown here was completely hidden by green plastic.

Left, bottom: The second lobby of the Karlton was adorned with white Italian marble wainscoting, violet Breche-marble pilasters between French-cut glass mirrors and three chandeliers of Venetian crystal.

Opposite, top: The Karlton Theatre foyer was decorated in marble, with gold-leaf and polychrome wall appliqué. On each side of the foyer were fountains of Bottechino marble above which were murals by George Harding (1882–1959). Similar fountains and many large murals by Harding appeared in the 1924 Earle Theatre, built by the same architectural firm.

Opposite, bottom: The Karlton provided another example of saving on expensive side-exit doors—this time with twelve doors exiting under the stage and behind the pipe-organ console. The side walls were paneled with imported French tapestry of dark green silk brocaded with gold. The wainscoting was Spanish leather and Circassian walnut. Cove lighting and crystal wall fixtures helped to relieve the tunnel effect created by 42 rows of seats. In its current incarnation as the Midtown Theatre, this auditorium has been twinned.

The Diamond Theatre

Above: The Diamond Theatre, 2119 Germantown Avenue, designed for silent pictures, opened in 1920. The original bulbed sign is still visible in this photo behind the 1937 marquee designed by architect David Supowitz (1893–1964).

Below: The wide cove-lit interior of the Diamond shown in this photo still displays evidence of the silent era: the ubiquitous artificial-flower baskets, illuminated clock and theater pipe organ—all anachronisms in 1937.

The Fox Theatre

Above: The Fox Theatre, at 16th and Market Streets, was the finest of only six theaters in Philadelphia designed by noted theater architect Thomas W. Lamb (1871–1942). The hexagonal box office was the city's most beautiful, with a French Alps green-marble base supporting hand-worked bronze pillars and grillwork surmounted by a heavy brass dome. The lobbies were contained in the office structure, which was built on the same design as Loew's State Theatre on Times Square in New York City. To the right in this drawing (from the January 1924 issue of *Architecture and Building*) is the Stanton Theatre. This Fox opened in 1923; the second Fox Theatre, at Broad and Locust Streets, opened four years later.

The Fox Theatre

Opposite, top: "The men's lounge approaches the bizzare [sic] in its interior treatment," was the comment accompanying this image in the January 1924 issue of *Architecture and Building*. The inset wall tiles display a tantalizing portion of a philosophical thought.

Opposite, bottom: The Fox's auditorium used 87,000 tons of marble, comprising 15 varieties, delineating a decorative scheme of old-rose brocade. The cove-lit center dome supported a large crystal chandelier, surrounded by 40 illuminated recesses. The projection booth was flush within the ceiling's curve and thus did not disturb the architectural treatment. The Fox's "Grand Orchestra" rivaled the Stanley's. The Fox's elegant stage shows were produced by staff, and in-house broadcasting facilities aired the programs twice weekly.

Above: This 1946 exterior shot shows crowds gathered for the world premiere of *Centennial Summer* at the Fox.

The Logan Theatre

Opposite, top: The Logan Theatre, 4732 North Broad Street, designed by architects Hoffman & Henon, was one of the largest of this firm's neighborhood theaters. All of the major Stanley-chain houses had these 20-foot-high "V"-shaped electric roof signs, which illuminated the entire block. The 1920s equivalent of the discotheque was the ballroom, and the Logan's was more luxurious than the theater itself. As seen in this photo, the fanlights could be tilted open for ventilation.

Opposite, bottom: The Logan's 1924 Adam design featured green marble and damask panels of wine, ivory and gold. The garden stage setting had decorative houses used as entrances for the entertainers. The theater used an organ (situated in the center of the orchestra pit) as accompaniment for the silent pictures.

The Earle Theatre

Above: The Earle Theatre, at the southeast corner of Eleventh and Market Streets, was designed by architects Hoffman & Henon. At the time of its 1924 opening, the Earle was the most expensive theater ever built in Philadelphia, and it looked it. This 1923 construction photograph, looking across Market Street, shows that the theater was originally called the Elrae (Earle spelled backwards). George H. Earle, Jr., after whom the theater was named, was a Stanley Corporation stockholder. His parents objected to having the family name used in a theatrical enterprise. Despite their reticence, the reversed name was ultimately dropped. Earle became Governor of Pennsylvania in 1935.

The Earle Theatre

Above: A huge electric roof sign atop the Earle Theatre originally flashed, "Keith Vaudeville." That attraction was replaced in the 1930s when this house became the city's leading "Big Band" theater.

Opposite: In lobby number two were five entranceways on the mezzanine, all leading to a large landing overlooking the foyer. Shown is one of the 27 murals placed throughout the theater and painted by Philadelphia artist George Harding. The abundance and vividness of the fine materials used is evidenced in this approach to the third open area of the spacious playhouse.

The Earle Theatre

Opposite: A closeup of the grand approach to the mezzanine level reveals the richness of the marble and the gold-leafed plaster reliefs. There were two additional impressive staircases from the foyer.

Left: The back wall of the foyer contained three major tapestries, impressively framed. Crystal wall brackets matching the central chandelier and stained-glass exit signs added to the ambience.

Below: A richly furnished promenade (with ramped access to the loges) and stairs to the first balcony overlooked the Earle's main-floor foyer.

The Earle Theatre

Above: The Earle's stage opening was 62 feet wide and 35 feet deep with a swimming pool below the first sub-basement—a holding tank for aquatic animal acts. Three stage lifts could move a bandstand to the footlights, close to the increasingly frenetic audiences. One reviewer commented, "Kids went rigid in their seats, while others danced in the aisles. We came back to the paper and said the show didn't call for a vaudeville reviewer, it needed a psychiatrist to appraise just what the hell was happening." The Earle Theatre remains in memory as the number-one live venue for pop stars from its inception to its demise in 1953.

The Felton Theatre

Above: The Felton Theatre, Rising Sun Avenue and Loudon Street, was built in 1919 but altered six years later by architects Magaziner, Eberhard & Harris. This was a small theater until 1925, when the architects cleverly tripled its size by extending the auditorium into a difficult triangular lot, squaring off the end of the auditorium and masking the stage into the resultant narrow confine. The Spanish Revival exterior shows imagination worked with concrete forms. *(Magaziner Collection, Athenaeum of Philadelphia.)*

Below: The Felton's organ chambers help to disguise the narrowness of its triangular corner. The Spanish-style hanging lanterns, plaster ceiling reliefs and rich-looking valances all contribute to a pleasant surrounding in this surprisingly large (1,362 seats) neighborhood movie theater. *(Magaziner Collection, Athenaeum of Philadelphia.)*

NEW·FORREST THEATRE

N.W. COR. 21ST AND MARKET STS

FOR MESSRS. A.L. ERLANGER
C.B. DILLINGHAM

HOFFMAN-HENON CO.
ARCHITECTS & ENGINEERS

The Erlanger Theatre

Above: The Erlanger Theatre, 21st and Market Streets (architects: Hoffman & Henon), was the city's most beautiful, elaborate and spacious legitimate theater when it opened on October 3, 1927. The theater as built deviated from this original artist's rendering in two significant regards. A "New Forrest" was built on Walnut Street the same year by architect Herbert Krapp, and the Erlanger's stage house was raised two stories to accommodate both a larger proscenium and increased stage depth.

Opposite: Abraham Lincoln Erlanger's long-standing interest in the architecture of Napoleonic France was represented in the decor of the Erlanger Theatre. Murals, such as those in lobby number three (shown here), the second lobby and the three lobby mezzanines, were created by Jules LeBoutelier. The staircase gave access to the English Hunt Room, the Jade Room and the Powder Room.

The Erlanger Theatre

Above: The Erlanger's Spanish Lounge was reached by two more elaborate staircases. Furnished with a wealth of rare paintings, vases and custom furniture, this large room resembled the grand salon of an ocean liner. As a smoking room for men (and women!) it was labeled "daring."

Opposite, top: The last row of seats in the Erlanger's balcony (above the lobbies) was 140 feet from the footlights. The large stage had freight and passenger elevators that serviced 24 dressing rooms.

Opposite, bottom: The Erlanger's upper balcony could be closed off, as shown here, to provide a more intimate setting for nonmusical shows.

The Town Hall Theatre

Above: The Town Hall Theatre, 150 North Broad Street, designed by architect Horace W. Castor (1870–1966), is perhaps best known as the Scottish Rite Temple. Built as a Masonic Hall in 1927, the building was sold in 1938 and operated as a theater and concert hall until 1970, when the Masons repurchased it. It was demolished in 1983. The architectural severity of the facade belies the rich detailing and ornamentation that appeared throughout the building. The third, fourth and fifth levels had slit windows, brilliantly illuminated from within. The spaces between the windows were pastel-lit from under the sixth-floor cornice. Caen stone walls and black channeled columns lined the 1,900-seat auditorium. A stage 45 feet deep with five lifts and a grid height of 105 feet made for an exceptional performance space. In addition, there was a 700-seat auditorium on the sixth level as well as a 1,200-seat ballroom on the seventh used by the Philadelphia Orchestra for rehearsals and recordings. *(Dillon Collection, Athenaeum of Philadelphia.)*

The Forrest Theatre

Opposite, top: The Forrest Theatre, Eleventh and Walnut Streets (architect: Herbert J. Krapp), replaced an earlier theater with the same name located at Broad and Sansom Streets in 1928. This architect's sketch shows a facade-length iron-and-glass canopy, a feature removed by order of the Philadelphia Art Jury in 1930. *(William Morrison Collection.)*

Opposite, bottom: The Forrest's interior was executed in an elegant Adam style. The wall-to-wall backstage measures 90 feet because the elevator-serviced separate dressing-room wing is approached via a tunnel under a small rear street. The Forrest quickly became, and remains, Philadelphia's leading legitimate theater. After the theater was restored in 1978, a Shubert representative proclaimed it "the finest musical comedy theatre . . . with one defect. It's in Philadelphia."

The Ogontz Theatre

Above: The Ogontz Theatre, 6033–35 Ogontz Avenue, opened in 1927 as the center of a neighborhood shopping strip. This drawing, by architects Magaziner, Eberhard & Harris, shows the firm's fondness for the Spanish Revival style in theater design. *(Magaziner Collection, Athenaeum of Philadelphia.)*

Below: This December 1926 photo shows the Ogontz as it nears completion.

The Carman Theatre

Above: The Carman Theatre, at Germantown and Allegheny Avenues, was designed by architect W. Ellis Groben (1883–1961). In 1920, William Carman opened a 600-seat theater on Germantown Avenue. Eight years later, Carman opened the pictured 2,200-seat theater just across the street, while continuing to operate the first as the Galard. The new Carman was the most elegant of all the theaters built in North Philadelphia. It was fitted with tiles and other ornaments from the Tunisian Building of the 1926 Sesquicentennial Exposition. The interior was designed as an ancient Moorish palace, with stuccoed walls, Saracenic arches, fountains and wrought-iron balustrades.

Left: This window detail shows the use of Tunisian tiles and marble in the facade. The recycled ornaments appeared throughout the building, and even in the pavement.

The Boyd Theatre

Above: The Boyd Theatre, 19th and Chestnut Streets (architects: Hoffman & Henon), was the only Art Deco first-run moving-picture theater erected in the city. This artist's rendering approximated the actual facade execution.

Opposite: The underside of the Boyd's marquee was crafted in swirls of crystallized glass, and illuminated from within. In June 1930, the Boyd's oversized vertical sign was removed by order of the Philadelphia Art Jury, which concurrently ordered removal of the 100-foot-wide French marquee of the new Forrest Theatre on Walnut Street. Variances are necessary for any overhanging signs on Chestnut and Walnut Streets.

The Boyd Theatre

Opposite, top: The staircase in the third lobby of the Boyd Theatre accessed the mezzanine lounges and the rear foyer of this "L"-shaped theater.

Opposite, bottom: Ceiling-height carved polychromatic mirrors dominate the Boyd's foyer. Staircases at each end access the mezzanine.

Above: The last five rows of the Boyd's orchestra section contained individual armchairs on stepped levels. The shallow but fully flown stage and elevator orchestra pit were used only once—on opening night, December 25, 1928.

The Commodore Theatre

Opposite, top: The Commodore Theatre, 43rd and Walnut Streets, was designed by architects Hoffman & Henon, and built in 1928 by the Ballinger Company. An unusual feature of the "L"-shaped Commodore is its blank wall facing a busy street. The roof sign shown in this architectural rendering was later replaced by the ubiquitous high and bright "V"-shaped sign when the Stanley Company purchased the theater. *(Ballinger Collection, Athenaeum of Philadelphia.)*

Opposite, bottom: The Commodore's lobby displayed Spanish Revival detailing throughout. *(Ballinger Collection, Athenaeum of Philadelphia.)*

The Sedgwick Theatre

Above: The Sedgwick Theatre, 7137 Germantown Avenue, was designed by architect William H. Lee and opened in 1928. The huge auditorium (1,636 seats on one floor) was originally designed with a balcony. When the upper floor was eliminated, the vertical proportions were not changed. The cloister-vaulted ceiling added to the resulting impression of the auditorium's immensity.

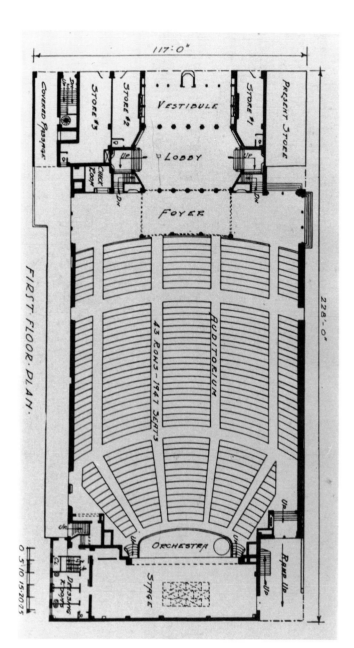

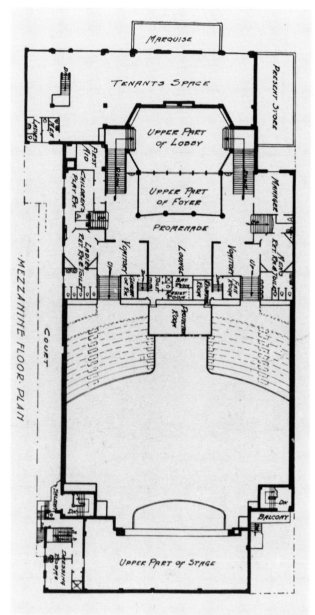

The State Theatre

Opposite: The State Theatre, 52nd and Chestnut Streets—Philadelphia's grandest art deco showplace—was the fruit of a collaborative effort by Thomas Lamb and Ralph Bencker (1883–1961). Each decorative element of the concave backdrop to the vertical name-sign was outlined in neon. The three building setbacks and the gold-leafed designs lining the cornice were cove-lit. Swirling lightbulbs on the marquee, the vertical sign and the secondary recessed signboard combined to create a dazzling presentation. (*Athenaeum of Philadelphia.*)

Above, left: The State's first-floor plan, with five seating sections of 43 rows, two elevators in the pit and a 100-foot-wide foyer, are evidences of an emerging extravagance. Coat Check, First Aid and Children's Play rooms were typical of the additional luxuries then afforded even in a neighborhood theater. (*Athenaeum of Philadelphia.*)

Above, right: The architects were unsuccessful in securing the property labeled "present store," thereby precluding a unified, symmetrical facade. The mezzanine floor plan shows the thrust-forward, "hidden" location of the projection room. This direct and short throw created a superior screen image and easy follow-spotlighting for stage shows, but it cost the owners 117 seats. (*Athenaeum of Philadelphia.*)

The State Theatre

Above, left: One of the two matching staircases to the State's mezzanine lounge had a landing wall of back-lit glass inserts in a blue-and-purple color scheme. *(Athenaeum of Philadelphia.)*

Above, right: The doors between the State's lobby and foyer were topped with ceiling-high glass panels and hung with Belgian-lace curtains. *(Athenaeum of Philadelphia.)*

Left: Back-lit polychrome Keppler relief-glass panels framed and supported the State's drinking fountains. *(Athenaeum of Philadelphia.)*

Opposite, top: Two of the ascending ceiling coves are visible in this photo of the rear of the State. The 32 recessed porthole spotlights in the balcony facing were becoming fashionable in the late 1920s, when the theater opened. *(Athenaeum of Philadelphia.)*

Opposite, bottom: The State's four lavish proscenium framings contained the organ's chambers and tone chute, as well as orchestra-pit lighting, two traveler curtains and one contour curtain in metallic cloth. *(Athenaeum of Philadelphia.)*

LONGITUDINAL SECTION

The Uptown Theatre

Opposite: The Uptown Theatre, 2240 North Broad Street, was the crowning achievement of architects Magaziner, Eberhard & Harris. The facade of the theater is essentially that of an ornate office building; East Indian influences are revealed in the upper window framing. The "V"-shaped sign, flood and cove-lighting, coupled with an ascending sunburst on the marquee, contribute to this eye-catching nighttime scene. The opening-night program described the theater as "An exquisite expression of twentieth century art. Grace of line, delicacy of coloring, beauty of craftsmanship, and the mystery of scintillating and reflecting surfaces." (*Magaziner Collection, Athenaeum of Philadelphia.*)

Above: This architectural drawing shows how Magaziner, Eberhard & Harris provided for generous lobby and circulation areas in the Uptown. The stage, a shallow 22 feet, reflects the changing concept of the necessity of having any *real* stage in large moving-picture theaters. Nevertheless, the Uptown successfully presented stage shows for 20 years after Philadelphia's last major vaudeville house, the Earle, closed. (*Magaziner Collection, Athenaeum of Philadelphia.*)

Right: The Uptown's spacious foyer prepared patrons for the high-style Art Deco auditorium within. (*Magaziner Collection, Athenaeum of Philadelphia.*)

The Uptown Theatre

Opposite, top: The Uptown's elegantly appointed promenade led from the foyer below to the balcony. *(Magaziner Collection, Athenaeum of Philadelphia.)*

Opposite, bottom: Just off the ladies' lounge was the Cosmetic Room, featured here. Note the makeup tables at the right and left. *(Magaziner Collection, Athenaeum of Philadelphia.)*

Above: A view toward the rear of the house shows the detail along the walls and balcony facing. Seats of striking pattern complemented the richness of color and design. The Uptown, one of the first theaters equipped with the newly invented acoustical tiles (built into the building's hollow walls), was recognized from the beginning for the superior acoustical quality of its auditorium. *(Magaziner Collection, Athenaeum of Philadelphia.)*

The Uptown Theatre

Opposite, top: Stylized capitals atop reeded columns in black and gold framed the six back-lit colored-glass bays in the Uptown. The color scheme was metallic, with lustres of silver, gold and bronze offset by black. The main chandelier was a central orb with rays of silver and gold. Marble wainscoting in the lobbies served as light-troughs to illuminate frescoes and grillwork. The Uptown was one of the most successful Art Deco interiors in the city. *(Magaziner Collection, Athenaeum of Philadelphia.)*

Opposite, bottom: The stage is almost lost in a sea of Art Deco detail in this view of the auditorium. *(Magaziner Collection, Athenaeum of Philadelphia.)*

The Circle Theatre

Above: The Circle Theatre, at 4662 Frankford Avenue, opened one day after the State Theatre, on August 30, 1929. This rendering, by architects Hoffman & Henon, complimented their ornate Spanish-style design by ignoring the theater's difficult location beneath the Frankford Elevated tracks.

The Circle Theatre

Above: The Circle was built literally in the shadows of the Frankford Elevated. The difficult location, however, did not inhibit the architects from executing an ornate Spanish-style facade in buff brick and ornamental terra-cotta.

Opposite, top: This construction photograph, taken from a passing train, shows some of the Spanish-style detailing that could be seen only from this height.

Opposite, bottom: This view, from above the platform of the Margaret-Orthodox El Station, indicates the tremendous size of the Circle Theatre, which was one full block in depth. The theater, one of Philadelphia's largest neighborhood houses, had a seating capacity of 2,991.

The Circle Theatre

Opposite, top: After passing through the Circle Theatre's large vestibule, a patron would enter this expanse of lobby.

Opposite, bottom: The mezzanine promenade overlooked the rear-orchestra standee area.

Above: The Circle was Philadelphia's only completely atmospheric theater. When movies were shown, the blue sky behind the side walls would come alive with twinkling stars in the forms of the constellations, while clouds would move slowly across the concave ceiling. This, combined with the elaborate three-dimensional side scenes—set five feet from the main walls with stained-glass windows, flowing fountains and lifelike trees—gave moviegoers the feeling of being out in the open night air of a Spanish courtyard.

The Mastbaum Memorial Theatre

Above: The Mastbaum Memorial Theatre, at 20th and Market Streets, was by far the largest and grandest theater built by the prolific theater architects Hoffman & Henon, with a seating capacity of 4,738. As this artist's rendering indicates, the theater was originally to be called the Jules, for Jules Mastbaum of the Stanley Company. With the exception of the name change, this rendering is an accurate representation of how the Mastbaum appeared when built.

Opposite, top: The Mastbaum was not only Philadelphia's largest theater: it was also the only one to occupy four street-frontages. This February 1929 photo was taken before the planting of formal gardens on the 20th Street side. The 20th Street facade extended 180 feet from Market Street to Pennsylvania Boulevard (Kennedy Boulevard); the "L"-shaped building contained five separate lobbies. Back-lit stained glass behind elaborate cast-iron scrollwork, floodlighting from above and hidden illumination from within the high projecting cornice added to the brilliant marquees. On the far left, at the corner of 21st Street, stands the Erlanger Theatre.

Opposite, bottom: The area below the orchestra floor, originally designed as a restaurant, became known as "The Grotto." This space became a repository, throughout the years, of artifacts saved from demolished theaters, including the consoles of forty pipe organs.

Overleaf, left: The marble railings of this Travertine staircase were of Breches Pavazzano, a rich white-and-purple Tuscany marble. The mural in lobby number two is one of hundreds of works of art throughout the Mastbaum, many purchased from the Metropolitan Museum of Art in New York.

Overleaf, right: Three sets of bronze doors opened onto the fourth lobby, also called the Grand Lobby. Behind the staircase was the lobby for the elevators, which served eight levels.

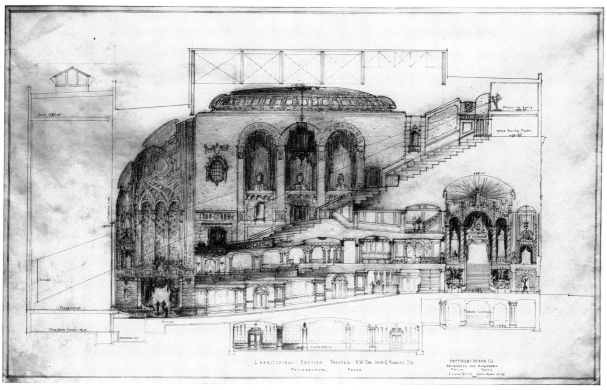

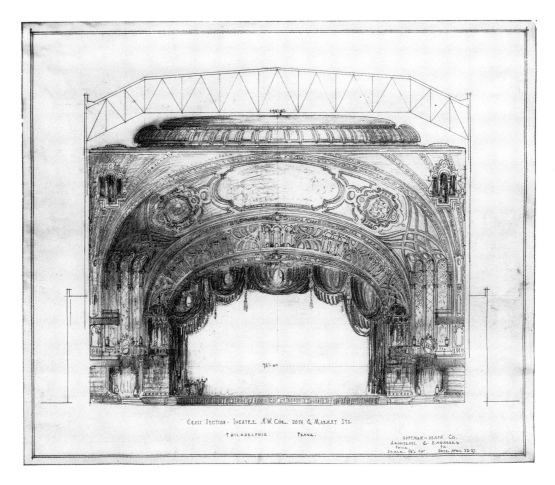

CROSS SECTION · THEATRE N.W. COR. 20TH & MARKET STS.
PHILADELPHIA   PENNA.

The Mastbaum Memorial Theatre

Opposite: This sweeping view across the five sections of a 43-row orchestra level gives ample evidence of the size of the Mastbaum's auditorium.

Above: Hoffman & Henon's original proposal for the proscenium called for Gothic-style tracery.

Below: Early photos confirm the use of a 200-piece orchestra employing three stage elevators and the orchestra pit. Arches, columns and railings were silhouette-lighted, and the pediments, ceiling arches and proscenium were cove-lit in pink and amber. The ornate hanging ceiling fixture disguised loudspeakers.

The Mastbaum Memorial Theatre

Opposite, top: The Mastbaum's main lounge, serving the orchestra floor, was bigger than most of today's theaters.

Opposite, bottom: The organ chambers consisted of three levels of components for the city's largest Wurlitzer.

Above: This side-wall detail of the fourth balcony level was described by the American Theatre Historical Society as "French Renaissance with a vengeance."

The Mastbaum Memorial Theatre

Above: Death of a Theater Palace. At the April 16, 1958, closing a spokesman for the Mastbaum stated, "this should not be regarded as the death knell of the theatre . . . ." Stanley Warner files, however, include an agreement with the wrecking company dated in March of the same year. Less than thirty years after its opening, the Mastbaum was a vacant lot.

The Midway Theatre

Above: The Midway Theatre, Kensington and Allegheny Avenues, was the last truly grand building of the motion-picture-palace era in Philadelphia. Opened on Christmas Eve, 1932, the Midway was one of the largest of Philadelphia's neighborhood theaters, with a seating capacity of 2,727. Shown here is a preliminary design for the Art Deco facade by Magaziner, Eberhard & Harris. *(Magaziner Collection, Athenaeum of Philadelphia.)*

The Midway Theatre

Above: This early sketch by Magaziner, Eberhard & Harris indicates the scale of the Midway, and how a theater could dominate a fairly ordinary streetscape. (*Magaziner Collection, Athenaeum of Philadelphia.*)

Right: The auditorium plan of the Midway shows how the theater was the central component of a larger retail complex. Provision in the plan for a "green room" and an organ chamber indicate that the theater was intended for stage-show use as well as motion pictures. The organ, however, was never installed, and for most of the theater's life the Midway's policy was strictly motion pictures. The theater was closed in 1977 and demolished two years later. A fast-food operation now stands on part of the site. (*Athenaeum of Philadelphia.*)

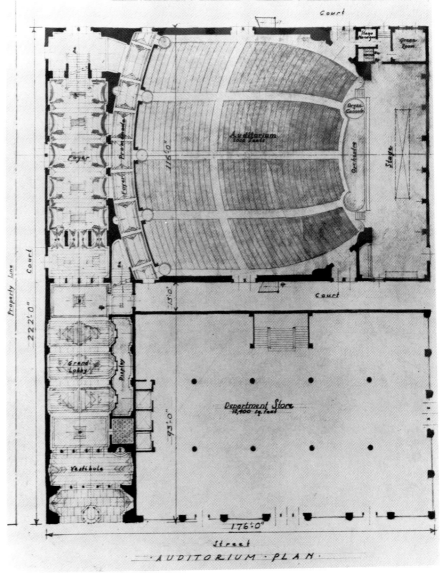

A Chronological List of Philadelphia Theaters

THE following list includes theater names, dates of operation, location and (where known) architect and auditorium capacity. Some well-known alternate names for theaters are given, but no effort has been made to present every possible theater name. For a more exhaustive compilation of data on the subject see Irvin R. Glazer, *Philadelphia Theatres, A–Z* (New York: Greenwood Press, 1986).

The theaters in this list are classified by type using the following abbreviations:

A = *Art and foreign motion picture theater*

C = *Concert hall, opera house or lecture hall*

D = *Repertory/dramatic theater*

E = *Variety theater (in earlier theaters, a predecessor form to vaudeville)*

I = *IMAX*

L = *Legitimate theater, play and musical venue*

M = *Motion-picture theater*

N = *Nickelodeon*

P = *Presentation house (presenting lavish stage shows and featuring a large house orchestra)*

S = *Motion-picture theater including stage shows*

T = *Twin/multiplex theater*

V = *Vaudeville house*

W = *Concert and sports complex*

NEW BOOTH [E]
(1724) Society Hill

PLUMSTED'S [L]
(1749–1758) Front & Pine

SOCIETY HILL [L]
(1759) South & Hancock
David Douglass, supervisor

SOUTHWARK (AMERICAN OPERA
HOUSE) [L]
(1766–1817) South & Apollo
David Douglass, supervisor

NORTHERN LIBERTIES [D]
(1790–1791) Front & Noble

CHESTNUT STREET [L]
(1793–1820) Sixth & Chestnut
Benjamin H. Latrobe (1805) / 1,165

RICKETT'S AMPHITHEATRE
(ART PANTHEON) [E]
(1795–1799) Sixth & Chestnut

LAILSON'S AMPHITHEATRE [E]
(1797) Fifth & Locust

WALNUT STREET [L]
(1809–   ) Ninth & Walnut
John Haviland (1828); Willis Hale
(1903); William H. Lee (1920) / 1,054

APOLLO STREET [L]
(1811) Apollo & South

McCOLGAN'S INTERNATIONAL [E]
(1812–1819) Eighth & Sansom

WASHINGTON HALL [C]
(1816–?) Third & Spruce
Robert Mills / 6,000

PRUNE STREET [L]
(1820–1830) 518 Locust

CHESTNUT STREET [L]
(1822–1855) Sixth & Chestnut
William Strickland / 1,100

MUSICAL FUND HALL [C]
(1824–1979) 806 Locust
William Strickland / 800

PENNSYLVANIA MUSEUM [C]
(1826) Eighth & Market

WASHINGTON MUSEUM [C]
(1826–1827) 48 Market

ARCH STREET [L]
(1828–1936) 609 Arch
William Strickland / 1,911

NORTHERN EXCHANGE [E]
(1834) Third below Green

PENNSYLVANIA [C]
(1836–1849) Second & Coates

NATIONAL [E]
(1837–1854) Ninth & Chestnut

CHINESE MUSEUM [C]
(1838–1854) Ninth & Sansom / 2,000

CONCERT HALL [C]
(1853–1894) 1217 Chestnut

CITY MUSEUM [E]
(1854–1890) 415 Callowhill

ELEVENTH STREET OPERA
HOUSE [E]
(1854–1911) Eleventh & Ranstead
850

LYCEUM [E]
(1854–1918)

MELODEON [E]
(1854–1861) Sixth & Chestnut

ACADEMY OF MUSIC [C]
(1857–   ) Broad & Locust
LeBrun & Runge / 2,938

COLUMBIA [E]
(1857–1912) 520 N. Third

LONG'S VARIETIES [E]
(1859–1900) 758 S. Third

AMPHITHEATRE [C]
(1863–1865) 12th & Market
Cardner & Hemmings

CHESTNUT STREET [L]
(1863–1917) 1211 Chestnut
John Crump / 1,189

AMATEUR DRAWING ROOM [C]
(1865–1882) 17th & Chestnut / 700

HORTICULTURAL HALL [C]
(1867–1917) 250 S. Broad
Frank M. Day / 1,050

SEVENTH STREET OPERA [E]
(1867–1883) 47 N. Seventh

PARK [E]
(1869–1968) Broad & Fairmount
J. McElfatrick / 1,694

CHESTNUT STREET OPERA
HOUSE [L]
(1870–1940) 1021 Chestnut
Bissell & Sinkler (1913) / 1,656

DUMONT'S [E]
(1870–1929) 900 Arch
George Plowman (1892)

FEDERAL HALL [C]
(1870–1901) 17th & Federal

TROCADERO [E]
(1870–   ) Tenth & Arch
Edwin F. Durang / 900

OLYMPIC [E]
(1873–1874) 1224 Market / 2,100

NATIONAL [E]
(1874–1916) Tenth & Callowhill
J. McElfatrick (1888) / 2,415

ADELPHIA [E]
(1876) Broad & Cherry / 300

BROAD [L]
(1876–1886) Broad & Cherry / 677

BROAD STREET [L]
(1876–1937) Broad & Locust
F. Loenholdt / 1,406

PARISIAN VARIETIES [E]
(1876–?) Eleventh & Wood

PARK THEATRE [L]
(1876–?) 17th & Ridge

FOREPAUGH'S [D]
(1877–1960) 253 N. Eighth
Wilson Brothers / 1,300

DOAK'S HALL [E]
(1880–1914) 1216 Moore

GERMANTOWN OPERA HOUSE [C]
(1883) 4900 Germantown

FRANKFORD OPERA [C]
(1885–1910) Paul & Unity

TEMPLE [L]
(1885–1886) 713 Chestnut / 2,200

YIDDISH [L]
(1887–1891) Fifth & Gaskill
Sauer & Hahn / 300

GRAND OPERA HOUSE
(NIXON'S GRAND) [C, S]
(1888–1940) Broad & Montgomery
George Plowman; Thomas Lamb
(1913); Hoffman & Henon (1923)
3,085

BIJOU [E]
(1889–1967) Eighth & Race
J. McElfatrick / 1,200

STANDARD [E]
(1889–1935) 1124 South
J. J. Hitchler / 1,500

PEOPLE'S [E]
(1890–1927) 2649 Kensington
George Plowman / 2,250

EMPIRE THEATRE [L]
(1891–1898) Broad & Locust
Willis G. Hale / 1,590

GIRARD AVENUE [S]
(1891–1964) 621 W. Girard
J. McElfatrick / 900

ST. GEORGE'S HALL [C]
(1891–1902) 1300 Arch
Thomas U. Walter / 542

GAYETY [E]
(1892–1953) 237 N. Eighth
George Plowman / 1,425

GILMORE'S AUDITORIUM [L]
(1893–1935) 809 Walnut
John D. Allen;
A. Sauer (1905) / 2,346

STANDARD [E]
(1893–1918) 4233 Frankford

MASK AND WIG [E]
(1894–   ) 310 S. Quince
Wilson Eyre

EMPIRE [D]
(1901–1928) 4650 Frankford
Nasehold & Knutzen (1909)

GARRICK [L]
(1901–1936) 1330 Chestnut
Willis G. Hale (lobbies);
J. McElfatrick (auditorium) / 1,561

TEATRO DELLE VARIETA [V]
(1901–?) 1032 S. Eighth

KEITH'S [V]
(1902–1971) 1116 Chestnut
Albert E. Westover / 2,273

BECKER [N]
(1904–1906) 20th & Mifflin
250

FAIRYLAND [N]
(1904–1908) 12th & Market / 105

MUSEE THEATRE [N]
(1904–1907) 127 N. Eighth

BECKER [N]
(1905–1927) 628 Moore / 300

EMPRESS [M]
(1905–1950) 1811 S. 17th
Hoffman & Henon (1914) / 490

FILBERT [N]
(1905–1919) 32 N. Eighth

LYRIC [L]
(1905–1937) Broad & Cherry
James H. Windrim / 1,629

EDISONIA [N]
(1906–1910) 210 N. Eighth

GERMAN [D]
(1906–?) Marshall & Girard
Carl Berger / 1,000

PALACE OF AMUSEMENT [N]
(1906–1908) 1019 Market

PERCIVAL'S [N]
(1906–1910) 50 N. Eighth / 350

ADELPHI [L]
(1907–1937) Broad & Cherry
James H. Windrim / 1,341

BECKER [N]
(1907–1916) 21st & Dickinson / 300

BIJOU DREAM [N]
(1907– ?) 1311 Market

BROADWAY [N]
(1907–1911) 716 S. Broad

COLONIAL [S]
(1907–1914) 15th & Chestnut / 600

COLUMBIA [N]
(1907–1910) 1328 Columbia

ELECTRIC [N]
(1907–1909) 2835 Germantown

ELECTRIC [N]
(1907–1909) 2709 Kensington

ELECTRIC [N]
(1907–1909) 64th & Germantown

ELECTRIC [N]
(1907–1909) Tenth & South

FORREST [L]
(1907–1927) Broad & Sansom
Marshall & Fox / 1,820

LUBIN'S [N]
(1907–1910) 926 Market

PLAZA [S]
(1907–1955) 2437 S. Broad
C. Oelschlager / 1,472

TEMPLE OF MARVEL [N]
(1907– ?) 3827 Fairmount / 150

TEMPLE OF MARVEL [N]
(1907– ?) Jefferson & Ridge / 150

AUDITORIUM [N]
(1908–1914) 2618 Germantown

BIJOU DREAM [N]
(1908–1910) Eighth & Market

BIJOU DREAM [N]
(1908–1910) 901 Market

BIJOU DREAM [M]
(1908–1914) 1205 Market

BIJOU DREAM [N]
(1908–1909) 1233 Market

DREAMLAND [N]
(1908–1930) 835 Market

DREAMLAND [N]
(1908–1911) 1217 Market

ELM [N]
(1908–1914) 2949 Kensington

FAMILY [M]
(1908–) 1311 Market
William H. Lee (1931) / 547

IDEAL [N]
(1908–1913) 2840 Germantown

IDEAL [N]
(1908–1915) 1829 S. 20th

KEYSTONE [N]
(1908–1910) 4813 Woodland

LEHIGH [M]
(1908–1929) 927 Lehigh / 499

LEO [M]
(1908–1927) 18th & Ridge / 250

LEONHARDT [N]
(1908–1911) 2905 N. Front

METROPOLITAN [N]
(1908–1915) 2042 N. Front

METROPOLITAN OPERA
HOUSE [C]
(1908–) Broad & Poplar
William McElfatrick / 3,482

MYSTIC MAZE [N]
(1908–1910) 2112 N. Front

NICETOWN AMUSEMENT [N]
(1908–1911) 4301 N. Eighth

PALACE [S]
(1908–1971) 1214 Market
Paul Henon (1911);
William H. Lee (1945) / 1,106

PEKIN [M]
(1908–1915) 2104 South

PENN ART [N]
(1908–1913) 2335 Ridge

SAN CARLOS [N]
(1908–1915) 811 Carpenter

SAVOY [M]
(1908–1948) 1211 Market
William H. Lee (1937) / 376

SHAMROCK [N]
(1908–1913) 1200 S. 20th

STATE [M]
(1908–1929) 2715 N. Fifth
Trepler & Heise (1924) / 450

STENTON AMUSEMENT [N]
(1908–1911) 2148 Stenton

SUN [M]
(1908–1925) 2728 Federal / 450

THEATRE OF THE LIVING ARTS
(TLA) [C]
(1908–) 334 South / 486

TUXEDO [M]
(1908–1952) 3949 Haverford / 499

ARCADE [N]
(1909–1917) 232 N. Eighth

AUDITORIUM [M]
(1909–1967) 215 N. Eighth / 416

BIJOU [N]
(1909–1914) 1931 S. Third

BROADWAY [N]
(1909–1914) 2506 Kensinton

CAMEO [M]
(1909–1955) 2940 Frankford
David Supowitz (1929) / 500

CRYSTAL PALACE [N]
(1909–1914) Fifth & Olney

CRYSTAL PALACE [N]
(1909–1914) 2916 N. Fifth

CRYSTAL PALACE [N]
(1909–1914) 2336 N. Front

CRYSTAL PALACE [N]
(1909–1914) 2618 Germantown

CRYSTAL PALACE [N]
(1909–1914) Seventh & Morris

ELECTRIC [M]
(1909–1924) 1038 S. Eighth

ELITE [N]
(1909–1924) 1630 Susquehanna

EMPIRE [N]
(1909–1913) 1111 Market

FAIRYLAND [N]
(1909–1913) 1319 Market

FAMILY [N]
(1909–1914) 1651 N. Eighth

FAMILY [N]
(1909–1914) 1236 Ridge

FRANKLIN [N]
(1909–1916) 3551 N. Fifth

GEM [N]
(1909–1912) 1532 W. Passyunk

GLEN [M]
(1909–1915) 463 Glenwood

GRAND SHOW [N]
(1909–1918) 3178 Richmond

HIPPODROME [M]
(1909–1930) 610 South
Hodgens & Hill (1925) / 505

KEYSTONE MARKET [N]
(1909–1912) 1203 N. Third

LYRIC [N]
(1909–1910) 2200 N. Broad

MAJESTIC [N]
(1909–1910) 5940 Haverford

MAJESTIC AMUSEMENT [N]
(1909–1915) 265 N. Eighth

MAMMOTH [M]
(1909–1937) 527 W. Girard / 700

MUSEE THEATRE PARLOR [N]
(1909–1914) 3064 Richmond

MYSTIC MAZE [N]
(1909–1915) 2242 Ridge

NORTH POLE [V]
(1909–1914) 1426 South

ORPHEUS [N]
(1909–1910) 5159 Haverford

PALACE [M]
(1909–1921) 222 E. Girard

PALACE [N]
(1909–1911) Kensington & "G"

PREMIER [N]
(1909–1913) 6011 Market

RISING SUN AMUSEMENT [N]
(1909–1910) 3417 Germantown

RIVOLI [M]
(1909–1970) 52nd & Sansom
J. Nasehold / 875

STARLIGHT [M]
(1909–1922) Fifth & Olney / 400

THEATORIUM [N]
(1909–1913) 1506 Point Breeze

TIOGA [N]
(1909– ?) 3524 Germantown

TWENTIETH CENTURY [N]
(1909– ?) 4314 Frankford

TWENTIETH CENTURY [N]
(1909–1914) 4258 Main

TWENTIETH CENTURY [N]
(1909– ?) 23rd & Master

VICTORIA [S]
(1909–1949) 913 Market
Stearns & Castor / 987

WEBSTER [N]
(1909–1910) 722 S. 52nd

WILLIAM PENN [S]
(1909–1931) 4063 Lancaster
Berger & Schmid / 3,230

ALHAMBRA [S]
(1910–1961) 1628 Passyunk
J. J. Anderson / 1,449

AURORA [M]
(1910–1914) 2132 Germantown / 490

AURORA [N]
(1910–1914) 624 Moore Street

BERKS [N]
(1910–1922) 22nd & Berks

BRISTOL PALACE [M]
(1910–1920) 4221 Germantown
Herman Miller (1914)

BROAD STREET PALACE [M]
(1910–1922) 525 S. Broad

CASINO [N]
(1910–1914) 3013 Frankford

CASINO [N]
(1910–1914) 4435 Frankford

CASINO [N]
(1910–1914) 2603 Germantown

CASINO [N]
(1910–1914) 4236 Main

CASINO [N]
(1910–1914) 926 Market

CASINO [N]
(1910–1914) 1209 N. 13th

CASTEL [M]
(1910–1915) 2211 Toronto / 450

COLONIAL [M]
(1910–1989) 1025 W. Moyamensing
954

COLOSSAL [N]
(1910–1913) 410 Girard

DRURY [M]
(1910–1934) 3440 N. 13th / 800

EMPIRE PALACE [M]
(1910–1914) 2846 Frankford

FAMILY [N]
(1910–1916) Ninth & Columbia

FRANKFORD HIPPODROME [N]
(1910–1916) 3054 Frankford

GEM [M]
(1910–1930) 1709 N. Croskey
Hodgens & Hill (1927) / 400

GEM [V]
(1910–1913) 1619 South

GERMANTOWN [M]
(1910–1953) 5508 Germantown
Druckenmiller & Stackhouse / 1,168

GLOBE [M]
(1910–1935) 5901 Market
Hoffman & Henon (1919) / 720

HAPPY HOUR [N]
(1910–1914) 2918 Wharton

IRIS [M]
(1910–1968) 3146 Kensington
M. J. Walsh / 1,400

LIBERTY [S]
(1910–1974) 1425 Columbia
Albert E. Westover / 1,635

LITTLE GRAND [N]
(1910–1914) 1719 N. Broad

LYRIC [N]
(1910–1914) 816 S. Tenth

MAGNET [M]
(1910–1915) 2616 Girard

MAMMOTH [M]
(1910–1913) 2500 "A"

MESSINA [M]
(1910–1922) 705 Christian / 248

MIDGET BIJOU [M]
(1910–1915) 41 S. 52nd

NIXON [S]
(1910–1984) 28 S. 52nd
J. D. Allen / 1,870

NON PAREIL [M]
(1910–1915) 3361 Kensington

ORIENTAL VAUDEVILLE [M]
(1910–1915) 7045 Woodland

PALACE [N]
(1910–1915) 2809 N. Fifth

PALACE [M]
(1910–1919) 2926 Richmond

PRINCESS [M]
(1910–1917) 508 South

SCENIC [N]
(1910–1915) 439 N. Second

TWENTY-NINTH STREET
PALACE [M]
(1910–1925) 2351 N. 29th

VIOLA [M]
(1910–1947) 2402 Germantown / 500

WHARTON STREET [N]
(1910–1919) 24th & Wharton

WOODLAND [N]
(1910–1914) 1497 S. 49th

ALEXANDER'S [N]
(1911–1914) 27th & Cumberland

AUDITORIUM [N]
(1911) 1627 Federal

AUDITORIUM [N]
(1911–1914) 1097 Germantown

AVENUE [M]
(1911–1964) 2713 Germantown
Albert E. Westover / 500

BREEZE [S]
(1911–1953) 1638 Point Breeze
Charles F. Schaef / 1,200

BROAD STREET [M]
(1911–1921) 3625 N. Broad / 904

CAYUGA [M]
(1911–1955) 4731 Germantown / 460

COLUMBIA [M]
(1911–1954) 2709 Columbia / 884

DORIS [M]
(1911–1955) 49th & Woodland / 775

ELECTRIC [N]
(1911–1912) Eighth & Washington

FLORENTINE HALL [M]
(1911–1914) 1923 Susquehanna

FRANKLIN [N]
(1911–1914) 1205 N. 52nd / 300

KEYSTONE [S]
(1911–1959) 1026 Lehigh
Albert E. Westover / 1,884

LYRIC AMUSEMENT [N]
(1911–1914) 1740 N. Croskey

LYRIC [M]
(1911–1936) 37 E. Main

MODEL [S]
(1911–1958) 425 South
William H. Lee (1930s) / 778

OLYMPIA [M]
(1911–1914) 1619 South

PALACE [N]
(1911–1915) 4254 Main

PASTIME [M]
(1911–1953) 1420 Point Breeze
E. Wilson (1923) / 800

PRINCESS [M]
(1911–1954) 1018 Market
Hoffman & Henon (1919) / 446

ROYAL PALACE [M]
(1911–1921) Girard & Crease

SEGAL'S [N]
(1911–1914) 1323 South

WOODLAND AVENUE PALACE [N]
(1911–1914) 6334 Woodland

ALLEGHENY [S]
(1912–1956) 3141 Frankford
Magaziner & Potter; Hoffman &
Henon (1926) / 2,855

AVENUE [N]
(1912–1914) 7282 Woodland

BECKER [N]
(1912–   ) Bouvier & Snyder / 499

COLONIAL [M]
(1912–1943) Lancaster & Aspen
Hodgens & Hill (1927) / 496

DIAMOND [N]
(1912) 2442 Frankford

DIXIE [M]
(1912–1953) 1224 Point Breeze / 450

ELITE [M]
(1912–1924) 5917 Torresdale / 247

FRANKLIN [M]
(1912–1931) 753 S. Third / 684

GIRARD AMUSEMENT [N]
(1912–1914) 2525 Girard

GRAND [M]
(1912–1962) Seventh & Snyder
William H. Lee (1937) / 850

GREAT NORTHERN [M]
(1912–1953) 3639 N. Broad
Henon & Boyle (1916) / 1,058

HOLLYWOOD [M]
(1912–1960) 2848 N. 22nd
Magaziner, Eberhard & Harris
(1928) / 499

HOWARD [N]
(1912–1913) 3405 N. Front

JUMBO [M]
(1912–1964) Front & Girard
Carl Berger / 1,300

KEYSTONE PICTURE [N]
(1912–1914) 2545 E. Dauphin

LEADER [S]
(1912–1968) 4102 Lancaster
John D. Allen / 988

LEHIGH [M]
(1912–1955) 2516 W. Lehigh
G. J. Reich / 490

LIBERTY [M]
(1912–1922) 3526 Longshore

LYCEUM [M]
(1912–1913) 6053 Ridge

MIRROR [N]
(1912–1913) Fifth & Reed

MONTGOMERY [M]
(1912–1936) 523 E. Girard / 650

NATIONAL PALACE [N]
(1912–1915) 1332 S. Fifth

NORRIS [M]
(1912–1947) 1826 W. Norris / 465

NORTH THEATRE
AUDITORIUM [M]
(1912–1915) 2805 Dauphin

OLYMPIA [M]
(1912–1929) 711 S. Broad / 500

ORPHEUM [S]
(1912–1967) 42 W. Chelten
John D. Allen;
Sauer & Hahn / 1,706

PALACE [M]
(1912–1921) 4140 Aspen

PALM [E]
(1912–1970) Frankford & Norris
R. Beard (1919) / 1,902

PLAYS & PLAYERS [L]
(1912–   ) 1714 Delancey
Amos W. Barnes / 336

PREMIER [M]
(1912–1931) 1320 Point Breeze
Charles Oelschlager (1915) / 460

SEGAL'S CASTLE [M]
(1912–1936) Frankford & Amber
Hoffman & Henon (1926) / 900

SENATE [M]
(1912–1962) 1710 Susquehanna / 500

SIXTIETH STREET [M]
(1912–1957) 456 N. 60th
H. Housekeeper / 475

STAR [N]
(1912–1914) 1628 Fountain

STAR [N]
(1912–1915) 2023 N. 17th

TACONY HIPPODROME [M]
(1912–1928) 3623 Longshore / 550

333 [M]
(1912–1955) 333 Market
W. H. Hoffman / 956

VERNON PLACE [M]
(1912–1914) 5704 Germantown
J. Allen

YORK [M]
(1912–1949) 26th & York
Hoffman & Henon (1927) / 790

AVOCA [N]
(1913–1914) 20th & McKean

BALTIMORE [M]
(1913–1938) 5026 Baltimore
N. Raidman / 460

BELGRADE [M]
(1913–1966) 2848 Belgrade
David Supowitz (1937) / 500

BRIDESBURG [M]
(1913–1933) 2747 Bridge / 498

BROADWAY [M]
(1913–1914) Broad & Race

BROADWAY [S]
(1913–1971) 2042 S. Broad
Albert E. Westover / 2,183

CAPITAL [M]
(1913–1993) 1237 N. 52nd
Thalheimer & Weitz / 1,185

CEDAR [M]
(1913–1965) 60th & Cedar / 868

CHAPMAN [M]
(1913–1920) 3943 Kensington

CLEAR PICTURE PARLOR [N]
(1913–1914) 3614 Longshore

COLONIAL [S]
(1913–1963) 5526 Germantown
Thomas Lamb / 2,552

COMIQUE [N]
(1913–1920) 2408 S. Broad
H. D. Prettyman

EUREKA [M]
(1913–1970) 40th & Market
Stearns & Castor / 450

FAIRMOUNT [S]
(1913–1959) 26th & Fairmount
Smith & Erricson / 1,243

FOREST [M]
(1913–1935) Ninth & Girard / 493

HAMILTON [M]
(1913–1967) 5928 Lansdowne
J. J. Anderson / 600

JEFFERSON [M]
(1913–1930) 2217 N. 29th
J. Allen / 935

JERRY [M]
(1913–1967) 2029 S. Third / 468

JOY [M]
(1913–1952) 51st & Haverford / 499

LAFAYETTE [M]
(1913–1939) 2914 Kensington / 1,364

LANCASTER [M]
(1913–1928) 4545 Lancaster
J. E. Jackson

LUZERNE [M]
(1913–1914) Old York Road

MORRIS [M]
(1913–1928) 835 Morris

OWL [M]
(1913–1928) 2300 Grays Ferry
M. Dickinson II / 499

PARK [M]
(1913–1927) 3235 Ridge / 1,000

PENN [M]
(1913–1956) 24th & Brown / 468

PHILADELPHIA PROJECTING [N]
(1913–1915) 44 N. Ninth

PHOTOPLAY [N]
(1913–1916) 1918 N. Front

PIKE [M]
(1913–1960) Sixth & Pike / 496

REGENT [M]
(1913–1980) 1632 Market
W. Burney / 416

RICHMOND [M]
(1913–1952) 3037 Richmond
Allen Wilson / 1,026

RITZ [M]
(1913–1950) Orthodox & Tacony
480

SHERWOOD [M]
(1913–1951) 54th & Baltimore / 471

SOMERSET NICKELODEON [N]
(1913–1914) 2775 Kensington

SPRUCE [M]
(1913–1965) 5949 Spruce / 485

STRAND [M]
(1913–1958) 12th & Girard
Stuckert & Sloan / 471

STRATFORD [M]
(1913–1963) 1443 S. Seventh / 600

TIVOLI [M]
(1913–1929) 1121 Fairmount
Stuckert & Sloan / 382

TOWNE [M]
(1913–1952) 4159 Germantown
Oliver Parry (1927) / 500

UNIQUE [M]
(1913–1953) 36th & Haverford / 900

VICTOR [M]
(1913–1925) 3954 N. Franklin / 475

ABC THEATRE [N]
(1914–1919) 3321 Chestnut
J. Anderson / 300

ALLEGHENY [M]
(1914–1960) 25th & Allegheny
General Construction Co. / 850

ALMA [M]
(1914–?) Kensington & Ontario
H. K. Kline / 480

ARCADE [N]
(1914–1918) 5226 Market / 199

BARTRAM [N]
(1914–1930) 1909 S. 55th
Leroy Rothschild / 494

BELL [N]
(1914–1929) 2907 N. Fifth
Fred Greisler / 400

BELMONT [M]
(1914–1970) 25 N. 52nd
J. Bright / 1,000

BELVEDERE [M]
(1914–1961) 8320 Germantown
William H. Lee (1936) / 550

BENSON [M]
(1914–1968) 6338 Woodland
J. J. Anderson / 499

BLUEBIRD [M]
(1914–1957) 2209 N. Broad
M. Dickinson / 499

BROADWAY [M]
(1914–1955) Front & York / 1,000

CADET [M]
(1914–1948) 3401 N. Second
S. Morrison / 679

CAMBRIA [M]
(1914–1968) 25th & Cambria / 850

CENTRAL [N]
(1914–1918) 412 Market / 500

CENTURY [M]
(1914–1983) Marshall & Erie
F. C. Koenig / 980

COLISEUM [M]
(1914–1964) 5915 Market
Hoffman & Henon (1916) / 1,100

CROSSKEYS [S]
(1914–1957) 5931 Market
Hoffman & Henon / 1,995

CROWN [N]
(1914–1916) 2726 Penn

DIXIE [N]
(1914) 6131 Ridge

DRUMPY [M]
(1914) Broad & Montgomery

FAIRHILL CHURCH [N]
(1914–1917) Sixth & Lehigh

FAY'S [S]
(1914–1964) 4032 Market
William H. Lee (alts.) / 1,826

FRANKFORD [S]
(1914–1955) 4711 Frankford
John D. Allen / 1,595

FROLIC [M]
(1914–1956) 52nd & Wyalusing / 500

GARDEN [M]
(1914–1916) 5300 Lansdowne / 500

GEM [M]
(1914–1954) 1632 Germantown / 411

GLOBE [S]
(1914–1929) Juniper & Market
Hoffman Company / 1,710

GLOBE [M]
(1914–1929) 1136 S. 17th
Leroy B. Rothschild / 455

GRAND [M]
(1914–1921) 5206 Market / 471

GREENWAY [M]
(1914–1964) 5130 Greenway / 690

HIPPO [M]
(1914–1918) Lehigh & Salmon
1,000

IDEAL [M]
(1914–1958) 2203 S. Sixth
H. Kline (1921) / 700

IMPERIAL [M]
(1914–1954) 219 S. 60th / 1,474

ITALIA [C]
(1914–1966) 733 Christian
A. Winters (1929) / 680

ITALIA [N]
(1914–1917) Eighth & Washington

JEFFRIES PHOTO [N]
(1914–1915) 5032 Ridge

LEMION'S PARLOR [M]
(1914–1918) 1517 Moyamensing

LINCOLN [M]
(1914–1919) Fifth & Christian
Fred Greisler / 500

LOCUST [M]
(1914–   ) 52nd & Locust
Stuckert & Sloan / 700

LYRIC [M]
(1914–1918) 1231 Columbia

LYRIC [M]
(1914–1971) 5123 Germantown
John Allen / 1,000

LYRIC [M]
(1914–1957) 201 Morris
R. P. Brodley / 372

MARCONI [N]
(1914–1916) 1218 S. Eighth

MOORE [N]
(1914–1915) 415 Moore

NEW DROP [N]
(1914–1916) 1034 Columbia

OVERBROOK [M]
(1914–1957) 6242 Haverford / 1,000

PHOTOPLAY [N]
(1914–1915) 52nd & Market

PICTURE [N]
(1914) 17th & McKean

RIALTO [M]
(1914–1957) 6153 Germantown
William H. Lee (alts.) / 834

RITZ [M]
(1914–1952) 1106 N. 40th / 499

RIVIERA [S]
(1914–1962) 4411 Main / 1,500

ROCKLAND [M]
(1914–1970) 4910 N. Broad
A. F. Schenck / 850

ROYAL PHOTOPLAY [N]
(1914– ?) 1346 Ridge

RUBY [M]
(1914–1927) 618 Market
Hoffman Company / 360

SOLO [M]
(1914–1929) Stenton & Wister

SOMERSET [M]
(1914–1925) 26th & Somerset / 495

SOUTHERN [M]
(1914–1952) 1412 S. Broad / 475

STANTON [M]
(1914–1980) 16th & Market
W. H. Hoffman / 1,457

STAR [M]
(1914– ?) 2640 Kensington
Carl Berger / 778

STAR [N]
(1914–1923) 1720 E. Passyunk / 248

STRAND [S]
(1914–1971) 3601 Germantown
Carl Berger / 1,679

TOWNE PLAYHOUSE [E]
(1914–1965) 4159 Germantown
Rudolph & Mellowdew / 500

TWENTIETH CENTURY [N]
(1914– ?) 1643 N. 27th

UPSAL [M]
(1914–1952) 6351 Germantown
Borzner & Wood / 470

VOGUE [M]
(1914–1953) 1905 W. Columbia / 499

WEST VINE SCENARIO [N]
(1914–1915) 5532 Vine

ARCADIA [M]
(1915–1978) 1529 Chestnut
Henon & Boyle / 500

BELLEVUE [M]
(1915–1932) 2212 N. Front / 830

BELLEVUE [N]
(1915–1916) 61st & Vine

BIJOU [N]
(1915–1919) 31st & Wilt

BROAD [M]
(1915–1971) 4813 N. Broad
Anderson & Haupt / 499

CRESCENT [N]
(1915–1916) 5107 Butler

DIXIE ROSE [S]
(1915–1935) 151 Levering / 950

DOUGLAS [M]
(1915–1945) 4410 Fairmount / 490

EAGLE [M]
(1915–1935) 2420 Kensington / 450

FORTY-SECOND STREET [M]
(1915–   )

ORIENT [M]
(1915–1954) 6149 Woodland
C. E. Futcher / 628

REGIS [M]
(1915–1953) 1526 Cumberland
Henon & Boyle / 500

TIOGA [S]
(1915–   ) 3542 N. 17th
Sauer & Hahn / 1,400

WALTON [M]
(1915–1974) 735 E. Chelten / 650

WISHART [M]
(1915–1967) 102 E. Allegheny
Kuhn & W. H. Lee / 904

FIFTY-SIXTH STREET [M]
(1916–1964) 56th & Delancey
Van Artsdalen / 760

POPLAR [M]
(1916–1950) 903 N. Sixth
Carl Berger / 858

BIJOU [N]
(1917–1920) 49th & Woodland

IDLE HOUR [M]
(1918–1921) Broad & Bainbridge

SHUBERT [L]
(1918–   ) 250 S. Broad
Herbert A. Krapp / 1,868

AURORA [M]
(1919–   ) 1097 Germantown / 600

BELL [M]
(1919–1953) 1310 S. 31st / 499

CAPITOL [M]
(1919–1954) 722 Market
Paul Henon / 562

EASTWICK [M]
(1919–1928) 84th & Eastwick / 350

EDGMONT [M]
(1919–1957) 4411 Edgmont / 400

ELK [M]
(1919–1930) 2501 Ridge / 500

FALLS [M]
(1919–1929) 120 Midvale / 480

FELTON [M]
(1919–   ) Rising Sun & Loudon
Magaziner, Eberhard & Harris / 1,362

HOLME [M]
(1919–1929) 7935 Frankford / 400

JACKSON [M]
(1919–1963) 513 Jackson
Neubauer & Supowitz / 1,083

KEYSTONE [M]
(1919–1947) 937 South
Joseph Levin / 490

LEGION [M]
(1919–1930) 1616 Orthodox / 1,000

LINCOLN [S]
(1919–1955) Broad & Lombard
1,400

NORTHEASTERN [M]
(1919–1958) 6031 Torresdale
W. H. Lee (alts.) / 950

OLNEY [M]
(1919–1925) 5613 N. Fifth / 499

PASCHALL [M]
(1919–1928) 7103 Woodland / 499

RIDGE AVENUE [M]
(1919–1952) 1734 Ridge / 780

STENTON [M]
(1919–1922) 6069 Stenton / 380

VENICE [M]
(1919–1952) 1727 Snyder / 700

WAYNE AVENUE [M]
(1919–1968) 4910 Wayne / 480

CARIOLA HALL [C]
(1920–1929) Seventh & Christian
750

CLEARFIELD [M]
(1920–1968) 2512 E. Clearfield / 735

DEWEY [M]
(1920–1939) Tenth & Snyder / 476

DUNLAP [M]
(1920–1927) 1032 N. Fourth
L. M. Shestack / 465

ELITE [M]
(1920–1945) 2716 Girard
Leroy Rothschild / 611

GALARD [M]
(1920–1929) 3226 Germantown / 600
PENN [M]
(1920–1951) 1426 S. Sixth / 600
ROYAL [S]
(1920–   ) 1524 South
Frank E. Hahn / 1,200
ALDINE [M]
(1921–   ) 19th & Chestnut
William Steel / 1,303
AMBASSADOR [M]
(1921–   ) 5542 Baltimore / 1,000
BOOKER [M]
(1921–1937) 1030 Fairmount / 500
CRESCENT [M]
(1921–1950) 84th & Eastwick
Armand Carroll / 800
FORTY-EIGHTH STREET [M]
(1921–?)
KARLTON [M]
(1921–   ) 1412 Chestnut
Hoffman & Henon / 1,066
LIBERTY [M]
(1921–1960) 6812 Torresdale / 1,484
LINDLEY [M]
(1921–1958) 4902 N. Fifth / 1,151
RITTENHOUSE [M]
(1921–1928) 5232 Haverford / 460
RITZ [M]
(1921–1952) Sixth & Hunting Park
499
STANLEY [P]
(1921–1973) 19th & Market
Hoffman & Henon / 2,916
ACE [M]
(1922–   ) 4204 Kensington
William H. Lee (1940) / 920
ADELPHI [M]
(1922–1965) 1453 N. 52nd / 483
AIRPORT [M]
(1922–1962) 7032 Elmwood / 500
ALCAZAR [M]
(1922–1925) 58th & Woodland / 480
GRANT [M]
(1922–1955) 4024 Girard
Hoffman & Henon / 798
LAWNDALE [M]
(1922–1964) Rising Sun & Fanshawe
Ballinger Co. / 1,217
BENN [M]
(1923–   ) 6316 Woodland
Philip Haibach Co. / 1,345
DIAMOND [M]
(1923–   ) 2119 Germantown
David Supowitz (1937) / 927
EARL [M]
(1923–1962) 28th & Reed
Burton Simon / 1,014
FOX [P]
(1923–1980) 16th & Market
Thomas Lamb / 2,423
GARDEN [S]
(1923–1938) Fourth & Spring Garden
1,000
HARROWGATE [M]
(1923–1954) 3421 Kensington / 1,013
IMPERIAL [M]
(1923–1954) 921 N. Second / 1,040

ALLEN [M]
(1924–1964) 1209 E. Chelten
H. C. Hodgens / 400
AVON [M]
(1924–1956) 2217 South
Tunis & Genther / 617
EARLE [S]
(1924–1953) Eleventh & Market
Hoffman & Henon / 2,768
LOGAN [S]
(1924–1964) 4732 N. Broad
Hoffman & Henon / 1,894
REX [M]
(1924–1957) Ridge & Oxford
Arnold H. Mueller / 475
COLNEY [M]
(1925–1958) 5621 N. Fifth
Hodgens & Hill / 1,985
COULTER [M]
(1925–1934) 312 W. Coulter / 500
HOWARD [M]
(1925–1953) 2614 N. Front / 900
LITTLE [A]
(1925–1934) 2222 Market / 219
NELSON [M]
(1926–1932) Tenth & Ritner
I. C. Manz / 380
QUEEN [M]
(1925–1930) 873 N. Ninth
J. Fieldstein
ROOSEVELT [M]
(1926–1962) 4739 Frankford
Hodgens & Hill / 1,901
ERLANGER [L]
(1927–1978) 21st & Market
Hoffman & Henon / 1,890
IRVINE AUDITORIUM [C]
(1927–   ) 34th & Spruce
Horace Trumbauer / 2,127
LENOX [M]
(1927–1962) 5410 Chester
David Supowitz / 994
LOCUST STREET [L]
(1927–1982) 1411 Locust / 1,580
LORRAINE [M]
(1927–1935) 1028 Fairmount
E. B. Medoff / 500
OGONTZ [S]
(1927–1988) 6033 Ogontz
Magaziner, Eberhard & Harris / 1,777
PARK [M]
(1927–1971) 31st & Diamond
William H. Lee / 1,654
PEARL [S]
(1927–1963) 2047 Ridge
J. K. Long / 1,400
PUBLIC LEDGER CONCERT [C]
(1927–1930) Sixth & Chestnut / 400
ROXY [M]
(1927–1981) 6189 Ridge
Ballinger Company / 1,800
TOWN HALL [C]
(1927–1983) 150 N. Broad
H. W. Castor / 1,972
ADMIRAL [M]
(1928–1976) 2806 N. Fifth
Hodgens & Hill / 1,340
BOYD [M]
(1928–   ) 19th & Chestnut
Hoffman & Henon / 2,350

BYRD [M]
(1928–1970) 47th & Baltimore
I. Levin / 1,800
CARMAN [S]
(1928–1978) Germantown &
Allegheny
W. E. Groben / 2,200
COMMODORE [M]
(1928–   ) 43rd & Walnut
Ballinger Co. / 1,105
FERN ROCK [S]
(1928–1992) 6017 N. Fifth
Hodgens & Hill / 1,289
FORREST [L]
(1928–   ) Eleventh & Walnut
Herbert Krapp / 1,889
FORUM [S]
(1928–   ) 5231 Frankford
William H. Lee / 1,777
JEFFRIES [M]
(1928–1953) 346 Connaroe / 500
KENT [S]
(1928–1989) 2649 Kensington
Hoffman & Henon / 1,932
LINDY [M]
(1928–1955) 6900 Elmwood
William H. Lee / 1,430
OXFORD [S]
(1928–1975) 7209 Rising Sun
Ellis Groben / 1,964
REXY [S]
(1928–1975) 517 South
Hodgens & Hill / 2,063
SEDGWICK [M]
(1928–1966) 7137 Germantown
William H. Lee / 1,636
WYNNE [M]
(1928–1955) 54th & Arlington
Hoffman & Henon / 1,763
CIRCLE [S]
(1929–   ) 4652 Frankford
Hoffman & Henon / 2,991
HOLME [S]
(1929–1951) 8049 Frankford
William H. Lee / 1,364
MASTBAUM [P]
(1929–1958) 20th & Market
Hoffman & Henon / 4,746
STATE [S]
(1929–1967) 52nd & Chestnut
Ralph Bencker / 3,170
UPTOWN [S]
(1929–   ) 2240 N. Broad
Magaziner, Eberhard & Harris / 2,146
BANDBOX [M]
(1930–   ) 20 E. Armat
C. S. Parker / 499
DUSE ART [L]
(1930) 1821 Ranstead
R. Sabatini
ERLEN [M]
(1930–   ) 1814 Cheltenham
William H. Lee;
Armand Carroll / 1,700
MUNICIPAL AUDITORIUM [W]
(1931–   ) Civic Center Boulevard
Philip Johnson / 13,500
ALDEN [M]
(1932–1965) 3641 Midvale / 750

MIDWAY [S]
(1932–1979) Kensington & Allegheny
Magaziner, Eberhard & Harris / 2,371

NEW WORLD FILMS [A]
(1932) 311 N. 16th

OLD ACADEMY PLAYHOUSE [D]
(1932–) 3544 Indian Queen / 125

GRANGE [M]
(1934–1970) 5717 N. Broad
Leroy Rothschild / 1,000

TRANS-LUX [M]
(1934–1993) 1519 Chestnut
Thomas Lamb / 493

BROMLEY [M]
(1935–1958) 5810 Old York
Thalheimer & Weitz / 952

CHELTEN [M]
(1935–1973) 1159 E. Chelten
Thalheimer & Weitz / 800

CITY LINE CENTER [M]
(1935–1979) 7600 City
William H. Lee / 1,000

REGAL [M]
(1935–1968) 5413 Oxford
C. Dingleman / 700

CASTOR [M]
(1936–1989) 6631 Castor / 446

CENTER [M]
(1936–1985) 1638 Market / 439

PRESIDENT [M]
(1936–1975) 23rd & Snyder / 1,000

CREST [M]
(1937–1986) 5800 Rising Sun
David Supowitz / 900

DANTE [M]
(1937–1962) 1212 S. Broad
Armand Carroll / 500

MAYFAIR [M]
(1937–1985) 7300 Frankford
David Supowitz / 1,009

NEWS [M]
(1937–1971) 1230 Market
William H. Lee / 400

RENEL [M]
(1937–1967) 7238 Ogontz
J. A. Nolan / 700

SAVOIA [M]
(1937–1965) 1709 S. Broad / 965

LANE [M]
(1938–1975) 67th & Broad
David Supowitz / 607

TEMPLE [M]
(1938–1952) 13th & Tioga / 500

WARDEN [C]
(1938–) 1920 Spruce
P. Bogert (1983) / 150

ASTOR [M]
(1940–1989) 722 W. Girard
John Eberson / 1,464

BORO [M]
(1940–1950) 6184 Ridge / 480

TYSON [M]
(1940–1987) Castor & Tyson
David Supowitz / 600

BENNER [M]
(1942–1985) 6056 Castor
David Supowitz / 450

DEVON [M]
(1946–) 6333 Frankford
Thalheimer & Weitz / 787

GOLDMAN [M]
(1946–1984) 15th & Chestnut
Supowitz & Lee / 1,300

WORLD [M]
(1946–1964) 1830 Market / 600

GREENHILL [M]
(1947–) 63rd & Lancaster / 500

MERBEN [M]
(1950–1977) 7145 Frankford
Shapiro & Magaziner / 2,100

PLAYHOUSE IN THE PARK [L]
(1952–?) Fairmount Park / 1,437

NORTHEAST [T]
(1955–) Roosevelt & Welsh
2,000

SOCIETY HILL PLAYHOUSE [L]
(1958–) 507 S. Eighth / 242

ANDORRA [T]
(1962–) Ridge & Henry

ORLEANS [T]
(1963–) Bleigh & Bustleton / 900

PHILADELPHIA PLAYHOUSE [L]
(1965–1991) Broad & Wood / 300

REGENCY [M]
(1966–1987) 16th & Chestnut
Thalheimer & Waltz / 1,200

1812 [M]
(1967–) 1812 Chestnut / 400

SPECTRUM [W]
(1967–) Broad & Pattison
19,000

STADIUM [M]
(1967–) 3300 S. Broad / 750

RITTENHOUSE SQUARE [M]
(1968–) 1907–11 Walnut / 750

DUCHESS [M]
(1969–1987) 1605 Chestnut
Thalheimer & Weitz / 460

DUKE [M]
(1969–1987) 1605 Chestnut
Thalheimer & Weitz / 460

MARK I [M]
(1970–?) 18th & Market / 611

HAROLD PRINCE [L]
(1971–) Zellerbach Center
37th & Walnut
Vincent Kling / 165

STAGE DOOR [M]
(1971–1980) 16th & Market / 495

ZELLERBACH [L]
(1971–) 37th & Walnut
Vincent Kling / 914

WORLD [M]
(1972–1978) 19th & Market / 500

FORUM [M]
(1975–) 22nd & Market / 250

ROXY [A]
(1975–) 2021 Sansom / 120

THREE ON THE CAMPUS [M]
(1975–) 40th & Walnut

MANN MUSIC CENTER [C]
(1976–) 52nd & Parkside / 3,934

RITZ [A]
(1976–) Dock & Walnut
Geddef Associates

PORT OF HISTORY MUSEUM
CONCERT HALL [C]
(1982–) Penn's Landing / 500

OLDE CITY CINEMAS [T]
(1987–) Front & Sansom

RITZ AT THE BOURSE [T]
(1990–) Fourth & Ranstead
Cope Linder

TUTTLEMAN OMNIVERSE
FRANKLIN INSTITUTE [I]
(1990–) 20th & Parkway / 350

FRANKLIN MILLS [T]
(1991–) Woodhaven & Knights

RIVERVIEW PLAZA [T]
(1991–) 1400 S. Delaware
J. K. Roller

Index

(References are to textual citations only and do not include the Chronological List of Theaters.)